RONDO

Cold War Backchannel

R.D. Taylor

Copyright © 2023

All Rights Reserved

ISBN: 978-1-916954-00-7

Dedication

This novel is dedicated to all of us who had, and still have, nightmares of nuclear war, especially those few whose personal actions sometimes prevent it.

About the Author

R. D. TAYLOR is a retired economist. He has an M.A. in political economy from the University of Toronto and did doctoral work and taught at the University of Pennsylvania.

Most of his career was in policy development as a Senior Policy Advisor in the Government of Canada and the Ontario Government, which drew upon and honed his writing skills. He began to write fiction in his 30s, and over the past 20 years, he has published a historical novel trilogy, A Prospect for Orenda, in addition to RONDO, and is currently working on three other novels, including a sequel to RONDO. He has learned to write a good story! He has also published non-fiction and essays.

He is an active volunteer, including a founding Board member of the Toronto Nature Stewards and Secretary-Treasurer of Toronto Community Hostel, a refugee shelter. He lives with his family in Richmond Hill, Ontario.

Author's Foreword

Many in my post-WWII generation had nightmares about hydrogen bombs far larger than those that incinerated Hiroshima and Nagasaki. Weapons that devastate our own cities, leaving terrible lingering death from the resulting radiation.

We shared a sense that the entire planet lived on the precipice of something both unimaginable and yet all too imaginable in our dreams. We lived through the worst of the nuclear balance of terror and its crazy, albeit seemingly saving strategy of mutually assured destruction (MAD)! What made us shiver more came frequently on the nightly news: the moves and countermoves, bluffs and counterbluffs of Russia and America, which presented the constant threat of fool-hardy first-strike attempts or unintended accidental nuclear war. Alas, a possibility that is still with us.

You wonder, did such an extreme possibility sometimes require Cold War backchannels to help prevent it? That is what I imagine with this story, perhaps not far from the truth. I simply put my experience and understanding of government and politics to use in writing it without any additional inside knowledge of the military intelligence community.

Cold War literature is replete with cold-hearted cynicism. In this novel, a group of determined warm-blooded idealists on the American side finds a few like-minded Soviet counterparts. Both sides of the backchannel secretly seek to avoid destabilizing the nuclear balance of terror during the dangerous strategic exigencies of nuclear diplomacy. They have already run it once under the technical development and control of the novel's hero – Simon Kiss.

Dr. Kiss is the opposite of Dr. Strangelove. He's a good piece of work. His computer-assisted strategic nuclear war gaming uses the most advanced social science of the time. He ran it effectively within and between American and Soviet military intelligence in 1980. He's hoping sometime – it seems always to be in the indefinite future - to use it for non-military global policy development.

It is 1983 – an epic Reagan-driven year in the cold war when the atomic scientists' doomsday clock gets the closest it has ever been to 12:00. Kiss, now in hos late twenties, has just slipped out of the tight Pentagon security noose around him and moved to Toronto where he can more independently test and develop his gaming – a system he calls Rondo – for ostensibly recreational purposes in the electronic arcade of the swanky new Worlds club there. But in 1983, with Star Wars looming, a second run of a backchannel nuclear war game is inevitable.

The adventures and misadventures of the new backchannel game entangle Kiss with challenging characters in his new life at Worlds - especially in his strengthening but conflicted relationship with Sabina Hurst, the boss' formidable daughter, whom he does not want to endanger in his own high-risk life. He also suffers from the twisted workings of his own personal backchannel – deeply repressed memories going back to conflicted loyalties and friendships in his college days and, ultimately, his own guilt about "selling out" to the Pentagon. The pressures build up in both Kiss' external war gaming and in his internal backchannel until they resolve in the novel's series of explosive climaxes.

As the inspiration for this novel, I wish to acknowledge the groundbreaking work of strategic conflict thinkers and peace strategists from the 1950s and 1960s, especially Anatol Rapoport, the social scientist who first subjected game theory to empirical testing, and the late Robert Axelrod, whose "Evolution of Cooperation" confirmed Rapaport's "tit far tat" solution as a way actors with opposing interests in a conflict can avoid huge mutual losses and learn to cooperate for better results. Let me also acknowledge the global nuclear horrors so well depicted in Neville Shute's 1957 novel, On the Beach, and in Herman Hahn's "Thinking about the Unthinkable," a 1960s book contemplating the actual waging of nuclear war - whatever its value otherwise, that book added to the general fear that an intolerable nuclear war was a possibility, as it remains to this day.

Let me only add that the novel is based on the wired technology of the time, and the novel's occasional technical content is written for a general reader.

Enjoy.

R.D. Taylor

Richmond Hill, Ontario

The argument that he was neither a spy nor a traitor, but an idealist, is not without merit. It may well be that he has done our country some service, if only in maintaining the Balance of Terror."

Winston Churchill,

Quotation in Douglas Sutherland, <u>The Fourth Man</u>

A Rondo is a musical composition during which the first part is repeated several times…often the musical setting of a rondeau is a game of hazard…

Definition (condensed) from

Chambers Twentieth Century Dictionary

Table of Contents

Dedication	3
About the Author	4
Author's Foreword	5
The Pentagon, May 1983	11

Part One: August 1983

Chapter 1	14
Chapter 2	23
Chapter 3	26
Chapter 4	32
Chapter 5	39

Part Two: Late August 1983

Chapter 6	49
Chapter 7	59
Chapter 8	64
Chapter 9	67
Chapter 10	75

Part Three: September 1983

Chapter 11	80
Chapter 12	88
Chapter 13	96
Chapter 14	105
Chapter 15	111

Chapter 16	120
Chapter 17	124
Chapter 18	128

Part Four: October 1983

Chapter 19	132
Chapter 20	136
Chapter 21	142
Chapter 22	150
Chapter 23	154
Chapter 24	166
Chapter 25	173
Chapter 26	183

Part Five: November 1983

Chapter 27	190
Chapter 28	192
Chapter 29	205
Chapter 30	218
Chapter 31	227
Chapter 32	234
Chapter 33	240
Chapter 34	252

Part Six: December 1983

Chapter 35	258
Chapter 36	264
Chapter 37	272

The Pentagon, May 1983

General Lamont Walker leaned across the table toward a younger man in civilian dress and growled, "We may want another kiss."

By 1983, the three-star General, known to everyone as "Big," was a big man in more ways than one. At a beefy six-foot-three, he reported directly to and sat on the Joint Chiefs of Staff Intelligence Committee. Despite his bigness - his four-star superiors often said that Walker may be big but was "very fast on his feet." Those not in the know often wondered why Walker chose to remain a three-star all these years. To that, he had always growled, "Three stars are still command and control, four is only command."

Walker did not seem to care that this top-secret meeting – unknown to the rest of the high-level military - was in the Pentagon. It was his own personal safe room, so it didn't matter if a top General was suggesting a kiss to another man.

Anyone in the know would realize he was talking to Dr. Simon Kiss.

Simon was unfazed. He was a slim young man, though as tall as Big. He pushed back his wispy hair and looked straight at the General.

"I don't think so. I have likely given you my last kiss. You are aware of the current situation. Under Reagan, it is unlikely we would get away with such a risky back channel with a few Soviet counterparts again or that the results would now be listened to even if we did. Any of us, and that includes you, could still go down hard, even executed for our secret little caper. Now get me out of here and back to Toronto, where I can at least continue quietly to test and improve the gaming system."

"Well, what we did in 1980 came on orders from higher up, even if they didn't know the order they signed. They ordered "all means possible" to feed our Soviet intelligence into American nuclear war gaming to counter any Soviet change in the nuclear balance. I interpreted the order a little imaginatively, is all, including we only disclosed to either side what would maintain the nuclear balance."

Simon, who had run the secret back channel in 1980 for Walker, not for the first time nodded his head in recognition of Walker's bold and dangerous initiative to keep the nuclear peace.

"The answer is still negative to my trying the backchannel again in the current context."

Walker concluded, "Okay. If you're not yet ready to give us another kiss, you can leave the Pentagon, but your next stop is Alexandria."

"Oh, for Pete's sake, the CIA has been through my comb hair by now."

"Well, for your sake, if not Pete's, you better hold up to their interrogations. They'll want you to tell them everything about the war games under recreational cover you are starting to play up there in Toronto at that new Worlds Club. And I'll have someone sitting in there, so you don't make any CIA side deals. And, if you do go back up there, you're still ours. You can develop better war gaming, but you're still ours, Simon. Do you completely understand that?"

"I already agreed to that. And you agreed I'm up there to make love, not war."

Part One:

August 1983

Chapter 1

Simon Kiss was air-borne over Ohio returning to Toronto from a conference in San Francisco. He was thinking about his parting shots with General Lamont at the Pentagon. He knew he was on a short leash. But Toronto had been a sweet solution.

His overall approach to war gaming and any other strategic gaming of deep long-term human conflict situations was directed at whether and how cooperative behaviour emerged over several 'moves' by the conflicting parties. Inevitably, that produced outcomes that gave better results to both sides than continuing purely competitive behaviour. He had written a seminal journal article, still suppressed by the Pentagon, that had provided some game theoretical basis for that. His multi-method approach to war gaming at the Pentagon made use of developments in several fields in social science. Over the last few years, it had converted some top generals to the value and realism of his strategic gaming approach. He himself had once said "In managing mutually damaging conflict, it is better a Mozart Rondo than a Wagnerian opera." Simon had later given the name "Rondo' to his system.

Simon looked out the window into blackness. The plane was passing through thick thunder clouds. The pilot announced the flight would be encountering strong turbulence for the rest of the flight to Toronto.

Simon tightened his grip on the seat arms, trying to keep a grip on himself. He was getting a bit dizzy. He knew that feeing. From previous experience, he knew he might black out. Like at university when he was told that Donna, a fellow student he was in love with, had been killed in a car accident.

As the turbulence began, he wondered if he would drop into that strange mental state he remembered from a few times before. It had never been good. It had been...

At that moment the plane suddenly dropped 10,000 feet. Some passengers hit the ceiling falling back dazed into their seats or onto the aisles of the wide body. There was some screaming for a few moments. The captain came on announcing they had flown through a severe wind shear but had regained normal. He continued that the same storm system had temporarily closed Pearson in Toronto and their flight had been re-routed to Montreal for a temporary stop-over.

The passenger next to Simon spoke to Simon but noticed he was not responding, merely looking blankly and became concerned her seat mate was suffering from shock. She was about to summon help for the man, when he seemed to come out of it.

Simon said, "Shit." And then gathering himself he apologized to her and said, "Sorry, I blanked out for a moment."

"Are you all right?"

"Yes. Yes, I'm okay now."

"The captain just announced it was a wind shear. I've heard about shears but that's the first one I've ever experienced. You?"

"Yes. Of course, a wind shear.".

Simon later had trouble recalling all that had happened after the re-routed airplane had landed at Mirabel, the huge underused international airport northwest of Montreal.

He had first wandered about the vast space of the terminal. He saw a row of phone booths, entered one and placed some phone calls. The only one he could remember later was to Worlds Club in Toronto that he would be late getting back. After that, still in a daze he eventually wandered into one of the restaurants.

To his surprise as he returned to his full senses, he spotted a familiar figure sitting alone at one of the booths. Ivan Tarasov was a Soviet scientist and Simon's secret back channel Soviet collaborator in the 1980 nuclear war game. He had been at the conference Simon had just attended in San Francisco.

"Ivan, we meet again, so soon." he had said in greeting.

"Hello again, Simon. We had to avoid each other in San Francisco. I'm waiting for a direct flight to Moscow. It's delayed another two hours. I thought you were headed back to Toronto."

"Re-routed here for a while – severe storms around Toronto."

"Well then, by all means, join me - we can order more tea."

"Yes, that's exactly what I could use at this moment."

He sat down as Tarasov waved to a waiter, ordered more tea and then excused himself and went to the washroom.

While Tarasov was gone, Simon tried to focus his thoughts about his Soviet friend. The intelligence community in the West was never comfortable with the fact that Ivan Tarasov usually attended the just below top security clearance academic conferences that Simon and other members of the war gaming intelligence and IT community routinely attended. Tarasov's presence meant sometimes discussion had to be limited and the papers delivered for discussion could not include anything specific going on under any of the secrecy wraps. Tarasov's most recent posting as the Soviet representative on the council of the International Civil Aviation Organization headquartered in Montreal seemed to everyone in the know to give him a convenient cover in North America for the secret back-channel role in contact with Americans he sometimes played in international intelligence for the Soviets.

Only Simon and a few people at the Pentagon knew about the back channel used in 1980 to bring off secret joint nuclear war-gaming. Even fewer knew that Tarasov had been the key contact with Simon. Simon had long since concluded that Tarasov had both Soviet and American protectors – people whom he knew could be as ruthless in the cause of a continued nuclear peace as the "hawks" who sometimes seemed to want to chance a nuclear war.

Simon, thinking how much that 'chance' governed human events, dug into his briefcase, and took out a pad of yellow foolscap. He unscrewed his fountain pen and rapidly filled the page with a long stream of numbers and letters.

When Tarasov came back, Simon simply said, "Learn anything new in San Francisco?"

"Yes. I learned you're still on the scene, Simon. I mean, it was general knowledge you left the U.S. and returned to Canada."

Simon shrugged. "You mean you thought I just went into happy early retirement up here. Ivan, I'm only 31. How about you. I heard you were kind of shut down.

"I still get paid to keep up to date. I attend the odd conference in computerized simulation, though now I get paid by the nice Canadian guy I work for at the International Civil Aviation Association here in Montreal."

Simon chuckled at the thought of Ivan being a civilian bureaucrat. "So, it looks like we're both still a bit in the game."

"Yes, so it seems. We shall invite you to our next gaming and simulation conference in Moskva."

"When is that?" Simon knew he would not be allowed by his agreement with the Americans to travel anywhere near the Soviet Union.

"That will be when the coltsfoot blooms, next May. Alas, it covers my country place. You could maybe stay with us – it is between St Petersburgh and Moscow. I'll be sure you get an invitation."

"Coltsfoot, huh. Sounds interesting. I'll keep that in mind" Simon made a mental note to check out the coltsfoot flower. Tarasov was already signaling a future code word to him for anything nuclear.

Tarasov continued, "It would be a lovely time there, but perhaps we can discuss meeting somewhere closer to you in these uncertain times? We did not get a safe moment like this to chat in San Francisco."

Simon decided to be direct. "Are you suggesting it's maybe time for another kiss?"

Tarasov said, "Well, that I'm not sure. I wasn't the highest placed on our side in the last one in 198, but they needed me technically and trusted me to manage all the information and not to compromise the back channel. But this time the back channel would I fear have to be, umm, further back."

"Why?"

"The Kremlin is simply too fearful of Reagan. This year he matched our intermediate missile emplacements in Europe, and he called our delightful Soviet Union an "evil empire." Then he announced an all-out strategic anti-missile defense initiative. All of that was destabilizing and has our side very jittery."

"I suppose they are right to be concerned. But let me get this clearer: are you saying some more joint gaming is not possible in these circumstances, even if it would be useful?"

"Again, not sure. The new fears in Moscow could make it very difficult replicating the work we did in 1980 together with a secure cover on the Soviet side. There may be only one General I could work with now on our side. I don't know; maybe I can get through to you a possibility. After all, you are in Canada now. Would it be feasible for the two of us somehow to work together out of Toronto?"

"Well, I am not through shaking off the Americans but I believe the same group of Generals wants another nuclear kiss. But I would also have to ensure there is enough support on our side to do anything out of Toronto in 1983 the way we did it in 1980 out of the Pentagon. The last time they mentioned another kiss was last month, just before I left permanently for Toronto.

They still watch me all the time. In Toronto, even in San Francisco. I'm expecting another call-in from the Pentagon quite soon. It may even be one-way for a while. And you are telling me that even if my Generals want to do another back game like we did in 1980 most of your people will not be available at any level?"

"All but one, and I can't really guarantee or rely on that in Moscow. Last time there were four others in on it, one right at the top."

Simon said, "Sometimes the fewer the better in guarding a secret. But I myself wouldn't dare do it without the cover of more than just one general. I've had two. Even so, if nuclear destabilizing pressures are building dangerously again maybe we may have to try to set up something on the side."

"I agree. Even an indirect side game could feed into the other side's moves anonymously as one of several possibilities in their existing internal war gaming. That's how we had to use the old back channel in its last stages when things got sensitive. I have one or two technical guys I can trust and as I say, one General who has a good sense of top Soviet strategic thinking who would feed a side game. I suspect the Soviet military will be wanting some fresh nuclear gaming of their own, quite soon."

"Give me a day to think about how we might work a side game. Can you delay your flight to Moscow for a few days?

"Yes, fortunately I am not flying back this time to report anything specifically or urgently. I'm flying back to visit the family farm. That can be delayed a few days."

"Can you be available for dinner here in Montreal tomorrow night? I can also arrange to stay over here another day. I can go visit my ailing Great Aunt Agafia."

"A good Russian name and unusual here – you wouldn't be referring to Agafia Kiselov, the Soviet spy during World War Two. I know she is here, indeed I see her from time to time. I can't believe I didn't know she was your aunt."

"My side had its name changed to 'Kiss' when they started to emigrate in 1906. She ended up in Canada as a Kiselov after World War II. She's nothing if not discrete."

"Well, well. Kiselov is your aunt. Small world. Okay. Sure. Let's meet at some place good but out of the way. I don't think I'm being followed these days; would you be?"

"Not here. As near as I can tell, the sudden flight diversion gives me some cover for a day or so. I will call my aunt. She's in a nursing home here in Montreal. I can say later she's doing poorly so I stay here for an extra day or two to check in on her."

Simon gave Ivan the address of a restaurant for the next night.

"Now I must call Toronto and arrange for my hotel and new flight reservations."

Simon gathered up his bulging briefcase, shook hands with Ivan, and was off down the massive hall. He went to the phone booths and made a hotel reservation at the Ritz for two nights. An hour later arrived by cab, checked in at the Ritz, got to his room and dropped into bed, falling asleep immediately.

He dreamed that he was trying to make a phone call from a booth, but the phone wouldn't work.

The next morning, he slept in. When he awoke, he took a long hot shower and then made some more Toronto calls to Worlds and to Sabina Hurst, Roy's daughter, apologizing that he would miss the next meeting of the committee she chaired that was organizing the first Halloween Ball at Worlds.

Despite Simon's best efforts, he could not avoid the strong feelings toward Sabina heating up within him.

"See you in a day or so, Sabina. Bye now."

After his calls, he went down to the lobby and noticed that the Palm Court, the hotel's famous indoor-outdoor dining room, was already open for lunch. He immediately took a table in an inner corner of the terrace where he could not be easily observed. The late August day was still warm but very fresh after the big storms had swept away the humidity the previous night. He opened a blank note pad in front of him, laid a pen beside it and ordered an espresso, indicating he would be ordering lunch later.

Simon needed to ensure he and Tarasov had a sound basis for a new back-channel game. He had to review how to work with the Pentagon, explaining that this time around his counterpart would have to find a neutral city because there was likely to be only one rogue Soviet General covering for the game higher up. With Simon in Toronto, that also seemed an appropriate city.

The overall result in 1980 reported eventually to President Carter and Premier Brezhnev. It found that no further moves by either side were needed to preserve the stable nuclear stalemate. It was not a trivial result – it had been based on the moves of senior military players on both sides.

By 1980, Simon had also developed an extra reliability check for his conflict gaming package – a psychological profile of each side's players. But that assumed several team players on each side. He could then base his report on a group of senior players facing more and less threatening moves and countermoves on both sides, weighted for each side's average risk-taking and other conflict behavior tendencies.

In 1980, he even had data on every individual player's ranked first and second preferences in filling out the pre-game personality questionnaires. He could report on how internally consensual or divisive each side's moves were, not just predict the most likely ones. That added considerably to the conflict gaming results that Simon was able to interpret and report, because the more internally divided a side was on its moves, the more erratic its potential choice of moves would be over a sequence of situations. For example, any deep personality conflicts within either side could defeat any logically consistent sequence of moves. That made it much more difficult for both sides to interpret each other and find safe stabilizing moves of their own.

But that had only been possible because each side had accepted Simon's behavioral pretesting so that he could better simulate the behavior of the "sides" of a nuclear conflict situation. The result—to maintain the nuclear balance—had been both strategically logical and psychologically convergent. He called that a fairly "deep" solution, much superior to playing "at" a game.

Simon wondered how to achieve such deep and non-trivial results in any new back game involving only one Soviet General. He wondered if he would simply have to say 'No,' to Tarasov.

Then it occurred to him: why not employ a control team in Toronto and then compare its results with those for the Soviet General? He jotted that idea down.

Chapter 2

Michael Keefe, Minister of Finance and Development, was the most powerful member of the Ontario Premier's Cabinet. His large shadow followed him down the hall from the arcade into the lounge of Worlds, the new up-town Toronto club.

There were still some boos coming from the Arcade—a popular Napoleonic war game had been suddenly shut down.

Keefe sought out one of the plush armchairs in the middle of the Lounge's big room. A waiter he did not recognize came over. He had only eaten an energy bar in the arcade since a big lunch that day, but he resisted a snack and asked only for a glass of port.

Normally, in company following dinner at the club, he was at this moment uncharacteristically alone in the lounge. After ordering the port and taking a few first sips, then downing it, he leaned over and placed a piece of paper on the coffee table. He studied it intently. On the paper were two lines he had jotted down in the Arcade in bold black ink, the first was "*Napoleon Disparu!*" followed by his copy of an error message he had not seen before, "*Core Access Denied.*"

After a few minutes contemplating his brief notes of the arcade incident, Keefe settled back deeply into his chair and redirected his gaze to the ceiling. Its spectacular plaster medallion had been sculpted on the club's opening day in swirls of champagne-mixed plaster and streaks of his own blood by one of Toronto's leading artists. Alas, the man had consumed most of the champagne and was himself plastered at the time. He had cut his arm with the trowel, and famously said as he staggered down the scaffold, "It will symbolize a lively club!"

That memory brought an inner smile to Keefe, distracting him from his concerns about the arcade.

His inner smile did not last long. Keefe's vision began to blur, and he began clutching his abdomen and breathing heavily. He struggled with the searing cramps, and then began rapidly rubbing his face. Within a few moments he was grabbing his chest, until with his mouth wide open, his head turned again upward to the ceiling. With one last convulsion, he slumped and died.

In the absence of the duty waiter, Powell, the club Porter, had been approaching Keefe with a second glass of port. He witnessed Keefe's last moments.

Powell was a famous raconteur and keen observer. He was the only observer of Minister Keefe's final moments. Powell, when first questioned by police arriving at the scene, was as usual, unable to comment without a bit of coloring.

"It happened rapidly," was the phrasing used by Powell. "Well, I don't know how long he had been suffering, but when I approached the Hon. Gentleman with a second glass of port, it was as if he took a decision to depart this plane, opened his mouth, looked heavenwards, and did so."

And now, because any attempt to suppress the news would have been futile, the news was flashing across television screens throughout Ontario

"Michael Keefe found dead in Toronto's Worlds club... Club Porter, only witness... Details at 11:00"

By 11:00, the news media could begin excitedly reporting not only the great man's death and the Porter's comment about it, but that the cause of death was "not yet determined."

With Keefe so central in the affairs of Ontario and its Toronto metropolis, the news had a devastating effect within and beyond the government. When, after the few details of his still unexplained death at Worlds were revealed, Powell's description of the Minister's passing contributed to a widespread notion that Keefe had indeed somehow contrived his own fate: decisiveness in life; decisiveness in death. It seemed a fitting summation of the man.

Chapter 3

Roy Hurst was already on the latest newly opened section of highway 404 when his car phone buzzed. The Manager of World's saying on Hurst's car phone, "Mr. Hurst, there's been a death at the club. Hold on to your steering wheel – I'm afraid it's Michael Keefe. Apparently just expired, sitting in the lounge tonight."

"My God," Hurst blurted. "I just had lunch there with him and his Deputy Minister today. What a terrible loss. What was the cause?"

"They don't know yet," Sarto repeated Powell's already famous description of the event.

Hurst grimaced.

"Powell is a little too quotable for the club's good sometimes. Is there any indication the club might be implicated, food or whatever?"

Sarto's reply was a bit huffily, since he presided over the club's celebrated chefs, "Well, no one else seems to have been so afflicted. You ate here yourself today."

"Yes, of course you're right Tony. With Keefe himself. Better consider any club-related possibilities though. Keefe spends – spent – a lot of time at the club. Was he exercising too strenuously or whatever? Stay in touch with the police. Let me know anything and if all else fails, I can have a word with the Chief. I did him a big favor last year. Let's not be the last to know the club has any alleged or real responsibility. You know what I mean, Tony?"

"Of course, Mr. Hurst."

"Good." Hurst considered going back to the club, but he was already well beyond the city and tired. "Call me at home if there's anything I should know tonight. And for Christ's sake, tell staff to button their lips. Answer only the questions asked by the police. Let's try not to make it any more of a story than it already is. I'll see you in the morning at 8:00. Hopefully, we'll know more by then. Good night, Tony."

Hurst turned on the car radio for a few minutes, but no new details were being released and he soon jabbed it off.

Hurst could hardly believe Keefe was dead, let alone at Worlds. Keefe had certainly seemed vigorous at lunch, rather more so than his languorous Deputy had been. It sounded like a coronary or a brain seizure, or something like that, but Keefe had told him at lunch that he was in the pink and that he had done better than he had for years on his annual fitness test the previous week.

Keefe attributed his good health to his rigorous workouts at Worlds. Hurst made a mental note to check with the Fitness Director at Worlds.

Hurst swung his black Le Baron off the end of the expressway and onto the now unlit regional road, Leslie Street, for his final few miles north, unable to keep thoughts of Keefe out of his head.

Keefe at lunch had laid out a deepening conflict within his Ministry—one so serious that the Premier and some senior Cabinet colleagues were already talking of breaking up the super Ministry. The policy issues and personality conflicts in MFD were tough ones. And the resulting conflicting alignments across the Ministry seemed to Keefe to require the very kind of organizational development workshop that Roy Hurst was the best at facilitating.

Hurst wondered about a conflict of interest. The Ministry had given Worlds a forgivable loan in exchange for an equity interest toward the development of its Rondo gaming software. Simon had persuaded MFD that his gaming could ultimately be adapted for use in public policy modeling and strategic decision making of all kinds and ultimately marketed to other governments and non-governmental organizations.

In return, MFD was given a tape of Simon Kiss' proprietary Rondo gaming methods and software under development for the historical war games played at Worlds. Simon had been uneasy about this because the arcade core program contained some of the methodology and coding he had used and was still being used for actual nuclear war gaming by the Pentagon. He was reassured the tape would be safe and only "gather dust" at MFD.

The elegantly lettered address on the entry gates of the Hurst estate at 15000 Leslie Street loomed up in Hurst's car headlights. It was a large Georgian-style new build, replacing an abandoned old farm house caught up for thirty years in estate battles among the descendants of the pioneer family that had settled on the property in 1810.

Hurst hadn't hesitated. The exurban countryside up here was still rolling countryside. It was dotted with horse farms and some big country estates of the wealthy. He was himself by then, from his own inheritance and business consulting success, a wealthy man. He had simply bought out all the claims on the pretty property and built the new house.

He turned into the estate's treed driveway. The headlights illuminated a mixed grove of century oaks and pine trees that framed the Lesliehurst Mansion itself. He nosed his car into one of its five garages. Inside the garage, Hurst did not get out of his car immediately. The only other car there was an old Land Rover he had once driven various family members through some of Africa and nearly all of Britain, France, and Italy.

As the empty garages attested, he had the place to himself on this night. Leandra, his wife and business associate, was at a conference in Niagara and would not be back until late the next day, after which they both looked forward to a long planned weekend together. Hurst thought for a moment about the importance of family in his life and how easy it is to miss the whole point, when you get caught up in other things.

He walked through the house to the library. The large library at the rear of the house served as Hurst's base of operations when he was at home. He had managed to line the room with a continuous system of yew wood shelves and cabinets picked up from an old Carolinas hotel by a Niagara antiques dealer who was also did some sourcing for the club. The west wall was mostly tall windowed doors opening onto a terrace, grounds and the hilly landscape beyond, now unseen in the night.

He went to the drinks cabinet, poured himself a cognac, held the snifter high in silent tribute to Keefe, quaffed it and put down the glass. There was still a bit of fire in the fireplace lit by the houseman to meet an unexpected chill in the late August night air, a cold snap between a departing heat wave and on-coming heat wave. He sat down beside the fireplace in a large dark brown leather wing chair, his favorite, and recalled more about his lunch with Keefe and his Deputy Minister.

Keefe had summarized the conflict in the Ministry as being between some techies who wanted Ontario to get on the leading edge of developing new computer technology versus those old hands trusting existing industry to computerize, only as the market required. The Deputy Minister said the conflict was intense and had got beyond his control. He indicated at lunch he had already told Keefe he would be very soon tendering his resignation.

Keefe chuckled. "Well time enough for that, but not until you have helped Hurst preside over a little more bloodletting than just your own."

Hurst had agreed to facilitate a two-day workshop session with the Ministry's executive staff. They had parted at lunch with warm handshakes.

Hurst went through his recorded phone messages including one from the Deputy Minister with some not very helpful direction for the workshop. The other messages were not essential and he was listening absently to the tape when it got to the last message. He noted that it was recorded at 8:45 that evening. It brought him back to the machine for a replay and then a second replay. It was Keefe's voice saying,

"It's Mike Keefe, Roy, about ten to nine. It's imperative that you try to contact me tonight. I'll be at the club until 10:00ish. You can reach me at my Toronto apartment by 11:00ish. It's 416-962-4337. Please try your best to get back to me."

Hurst let the shock wear off, and then picked up the phone as if to make the symbolic call.

As he put down the phone, it lit up again and rang.

"Hurst, here."

"It's Tony, Mr. Hurst. The police took away Keefe's port glass and my police sources already say that they are rushing the postmortem and they have to allow for the possibility there may have been some kind of poison involved. I mean, possibly from Keefe's glass – they're testing it.

'Oh, shit! Let's hope that's just routine "

"I hope, but there's more. When they asked to speak to the waiter who went missing - Johnny Russo – he's our new guy - I told them he'd left without notice and a half-hour before he was supposed to leave. I called him after they'd gone, and his dad said his son hadn't come home. The guy seems to have disappeared. I'm very, very sorry Mr. Hurst. I may have failed in hiring this guy."

"If that's true, well, you know, the guy's name is Russo, maybe it's even some kind of a hit – I can't believe something like that happened at Worlds."

"Yes, unbelievable."

"Well, let's not jump to conclusions, but how did you come to hire this new guy?"

"Russo came with excellent references from two top restaurants." He mentioned the names.

Keefe winced at the name of the last one. "Tony, surely you know "Profito Rolls" is a place that attracts, well a rather mixed crowd."

'Well, sir, as for the mixed crowd, sure there are some connected guys who sometimes eat there, but only a few of the very top ones who expected and insisted on the city's best Italian cuisine when they did. I never thought they controlled the place. I mean, how many times do I have to explain Italians in Toronto are much more than the mob scene?"

"Of course, Tony, I spoke carelessly. I am perfectly aware that Italians have helped make Toronto a much better city than it was before the war. You may not be perfect, like us WASPs, but you are one of the world's greatest cultures."

"Well, we have also agreed that Brits and Italians are equals in being insufferable at times. Not to speak of all the others." They both chuckled at the long standing Churchill reference between them to poke at each other's ethnic stereotypes.

Hurst said, "Well, blimey, Tony, I'll have to be in tomorrow at 7:00 a.m. See you then."

"Ciao, and good night, sir. I'm truly sorry this happened. Something may have got by me."

"If so, I suspect you're not the only one something 'got by'."

Chapter 4

Simon, lunching on the terrace at the Ritz in Montreal, watched as an elderly woman in a fur wrap was seated at the table next to him. He smiled at her, thinking of his aunt. She gave him a severe look. A younger man very well dressed slipped in at her table. She gave him an equally severe look. Simon distinctly heard him say "Auntie, you look well."

Okay, maybe that's a sign – same old, same old, Simon thought.

He ordered a lobster salad, with a glass of Montrachet.

He jotted down 'Toronto?' On his yellow notepad. If the back channel was Toronto or near Toronto, rather than suburban D.C. as it had been in 1980, what other differences might that make? It would probably make the American collaborators more than a bit nervous. But maybe it would be better cover for Tarasov. Maybe now, though, it would also be better cover for the two collaborating generals at the Pentagon.

Simon sat for a half hour mulling over various approaches to a secure game out of Toronto jotting down various notes on what was done in 1980 and what could be done in 1983. At least the logistics of the long-distance data exchange could now be done via telephone lines, not just via a physical exchange of diskettes as in 1980, via couriers who could be compromised or followed.

As Simon thought it over the situation, it was more important this time to feed Soviet counter-moves to the Americans than match that in the other direction. The Americans had already recently made some opening and countering moves in their actual nuclear actions and statements. American leaders this time needed some reigning in – that could happen if and as they saw in simulation how their actual recent moves might be seriously destabilizing for the Soviets. Much would depend on getting something from the Soviet side via Tarasov.

Simon smiled inwardly. In Moscow, the more top people in league, the easier it is to shut things up; in Washington, the more top people in league, the greater the chance things could be leaked and blow wide open. It was an intriguing asymmetry between a democratic Washington and a not so democratic Moscow he had been thinking about for a while.

After lunch, Simon hailed a cab and went to his aunt's nursing home, a huge rambling stone building spread out along Sherbrook Street below Westmount. She was waiting for him, seated on a bench in its gardens.

"Auntie, you look well." She did look well at 76, though there was a wheel chair beside the bench.

"Simon, my good nephew, though not necessarily my favorite!"

They kissed.

"That's because you don't visit me. I am pleasantly surprised. What brings you here?"

"Well, there you are: figuring things out before anyone else. The Kiss imperative, I guess."

"So, we are smart. You know our family name, from the shtetl, it is not a Jewish name. That was deliberate choice of my grandfather, back then, just out of his service as a Cossack. He'd told us that we would henceforth take the name of a brave Cossack he served with who had been killed beside him. He'd said that way we can be Jewish and maybe not suffer so much in a pogrom. His wife told him, "So your name will be Shmuel Kiselov. That won't save you for very long." He said to her, "Maybe just long enough."

Grampa had been right. The family got out just in time—my side went to Moskva, the rest to America and Canada. Then me, later. After the War."

Simon smiled at the old family story.

"And brought with you enough contacts in Eastern Europe and Russia to be visited once a month by Canadian intelligence for a briefing on the Soviet situation. Do they still come?"

She nodded and smiled, "Don't tell anybody."

"Okay, I have a question now that I hope I'm back in your good graces: if one smart Russian in the Kremlin – perhaps a very senior General - wants to send some coded personal messages to the west could he use the new telephone data links to do so without detection?"

She thought for a minute. "Maybe. I just heard from an old friend at Northern Electric that those kind of data lines now reach into Moscow and St Petersburgh, but not so many I would guess that most non-authorized traffic could be monitored closely. I would think the General or whomever would have to use a telephone connection out of East Germany where there are a few independently secure situations. If I had to, I might be able to get you a list."

"Hmm. Perhaps we could get my um, contact a list."

She shrugged. "In my time there he would have an equal chance of surviving with everyone else, because no one was surviving then, whatever their loyalty or activities."

He nodded but still looked searchingly at her.

"What else," she said?

"What do you know about the unity of the current Soviet establishment?"

"Why should I know anything about that? I haven't been in Europe or Russia for thirty years."

"Doesn't my friend Ivan Tarasov come to see you?"

"Well, Ivan once told me he is your friend, too. Ask him then."

"Even he doesn't have your sources and perspective, Auntie. Let me ask you: how does the Soviet situation at the center now compare with say, 1980?"

"Okay, Simon, okay. You force me to tell you things. I do try to keep up to date. I do keep up with my sources. They are all now much older and therefore disregarded. But we keep up, it keeps our wits. Anyway, I think there is a big difference. As late as 1980 everything there was safely centralized for all of the elites. But I hear that it's not like that there now, because no one knows or can decide what to do. It has become weaker at the center – different groups with different ideas. This is now a much less stable situation for the Soviets than it was, even three years ago. Kind of scary today around Moscow."

Simon thought about how the asymmetric situation had also evolved in Washington since 1980. Then, in contrast to the Soviet Union, Washington was kind of safely de-centralized under Carter. The elites were busy doing their own thing. Mostly in concert. Now, it was different under Reagan. Increased centralization in Washington can be destabilizing because it interferes with the elites doing their own thing and working out compromises with each other. Centralized power forces greater conflict in Washington.

"That Soviet disunity now because central power is weaker is important for me to know, doing what I do."

"What is it that you do, Simon? You have never explained it to me."

"That's just as well, Great Auntie. I don't want you being pushed into the traffic on Sherbrooke Street."

"Alright, I won't pry. Anyway, how's your love life. You're not a kid any more Simon."

"Better than I deserve, actually."

"You need a good woman. But I'm getting tired now. Please wheel me in for my afternoon nap. And do come to see me more often."

"Yes, Great Auntie."

Simon got back to his hotel and took a walk west from the Ritz along Sherbrooke Street. He ducked into Holt Renfrew and bought a dressy shirt for the evening with Ivan. Then he headed down Crescent Street, which offered sometimes up to three floor levels, a wide range of outdoor as well as indoor food, drink and entertainment twenty-four hours a day in the warm months.

Simon loved Montreal. As he sipped an espresso at a coffee bar, he could hear the music of a Quebecois folk guitarist above the other street music and smelled the fish being grilled at the Greek restaurant next door. He wondered if his walk would change his mind on anything, or bring new thoughts, but it didn't – it just made him feel better. The world was still so worthwhile here. French Canadian joie de vivre was something even the English in Montreal now marveled at, finally accepting it as a mainly French speaking city and not just their own low-wage Better-Speak-English imperial plaything, the joie got even better as you got further into French Montreal, say along the boundary road of Rue St Denis, where he would be dining that night.

In the early evening he summoned a taxi and gave the name of the restaurant, *Graisse Moroc*, in English literally, Morocco Drippings for the address Tarasov gave him. At 6:30, the taxi dropped him there. The restaurant was not yet busy when he entered, and he saw Tarasov at a rear table.

Ivan spread his big hands with a big smile, welcoming Simon. He already had a bottle of wine at the table. "This is a particularly good Cotes du Rhone and it goes well with the delicious dripped lamb dishes here."

"The *'Graise,'* in the name?"

"Exactly. The place is actually owned by a Moroccan Jewish family."

Simon was not surprised. He knew there were a lot of French-speaking Moroccan Jews in Montreal. The waiter poured Simon a glass of wine and withdrew.

"I've told him we will order in a while. So, what do you think?"

"Good restaurant choice. And obviously, we need to be very careful this time. Things have been changing in Moscow and Washington. Have you confirmed if your side will be doing any strategic gaming on their own? I mean I know the Yanks will, but you need to be very sure about the Kremlin?"

"My contact is basically left alone, but he still has a say and a good ear. He tells me they are most certainly going to be doing strategic nuclear gaming now that things are heating up badly with Reagan in power."

"How feasible is it for us to update it for the Soviet side – the Americans have asked me to, and I have revised a lot of the program, with the latest psychological data set."

"Okay, I think maybe we say nothing about updating. If I can simply say to the remaining General that it would be advantageous to do again what we did in 1980, then maybe that would be best. You know what I am saying?"

"Yes. Keep it simple. He won't know it's been changed and improved and that, as in 1980, this back game is only to ensure the nuclear balance is maintained or not destabilized to either side's advantage."

"I think more and more Soviet leaders realize that any change to the current "balance" advantages America. That is why they are upset that the Americans under Reagan have been tempted to make yet another provocative move. I have learned that they plan to game among themselves a full repertoire of disruptive countermoves."

"Well, we had some in 1980 that were also designed to deter any future ABM moves by either side. But that was just part of a logical menu of moves - now it's the real thing." They reviewed in more detail what they had achieved together in 1980.

Simon then said, "Okay. I think I now have a secure way of calling you and for sending the data for exchange through the telephone system here and into and out of East Germany. A slow but secure process. They have our latest Northern Telecom digital switch phone installations and workers there. Can you give me a safe code for trusting your replies?"

Ivan said, "Here is my return code, so you will know it. No one in Moscow seems to have been trying to get at it, so it is still valid. But your warning about that is well taken. I won't be able to do much out of Russia itself."

Simon handed Ivan a page of dense numbers and letters. "Here is my new security password arrangement. The password itself changes daily and on a given day it will take you a bit of time to get at. I assume you will figure out the day code I will use if I contact you."

"Good. I cannot emphasize enough that I think the only way some of the sharper Soviet nuclear strategists see left is to cause some havoc which will bring things back to something more equally negotiable with the Americans."

"I was afraid of that."

Simon returned to the Ritz pondering Ivan's warning of "some havoc" as a potential Soviet countermove to Reagan's current moves.

Chapter 5

Roy Hurst sat down at the desk in his office at Worlds at 7:05 the morning following Keefe's death at the club. He sipped a freshly brewed cappuccino.

Tony Sarto was downing his second espresso. Not for the first time, Sarto wondered how someone as big and fleshy as Hurst could summon such enormous mental energy and physical endurance. Sarto, like most people, attributed Hurst's unusual energies to "genetics."

Then spent much of the morning reviewing the Keefe situation, waiting for a summons and/or announcement from the Toronto Police Department.

By 11:00, Sarto had found out from his police sources that the postmortem had been completed with the "immediate" cause of death being a sudden heart failure. They had not yet checked Keefe's medical record but expected to have done so by 2:00 in the afternoon, at which time they were now re-scheduled to have a press conference.

In the meantime, three detectives had arrived at the club and were doing a meticulous second search of the club's arcade. The room had been taped off and the club closed until further notice.

It didn't look good for the club. If there was a possibility that Keefe had been fatally poisoned at the club, it certainly did not look good that there was still no trace of the missing waiter who had served Keefe with the last thing he had ingested. Sarto had made further calls to the man's family, but they were as mystified as anyone about their son's whereabouts. It wouldn't take long for an active police investigation to enflame public opinion into believing a criminal hit had occurred at the club. And that would not soon be forgotten in the minds of current and prospective club members. The immediate temporary closure didn't bother him so much. As he said to Sarto, "It may take us a few days to persuade even our most ardent members they can order a safe drink here."

Sarto showed Hurst a draft damage-control statement that he thought should go out to the media, should the worst be confirmed about Keefe's death. It was an apology for insufficient security and new measures the club would take to prevent whatever happened at Worlds from ever happening again.

Hurst demurred. "Tony, in the eventuality that a poisoning occurred here, I think we're just one of the victims. It's more a question this happened to a very important person who happened to be a member of the club. It could have happened at any other of his clubs. Worlds happened to be where it happened. Me, I think we should emphasize our full cooperation with the police but play it down as anything at all attributable to the club - I'm going to assume, unless informed otherwise that our Ernesto is missing for another reason. Here's my changes along those lines."

He handed back to Sarto a marked-up damage control statement.

"Okay, I see your point. I'll get it out after the police press conference at 2:00. Oh, and I forgot to mention that the police are now scheduled to be here at 10:30 tomorrow morning for more staff interviews. They will use the lounge, I guess. I'll inform staff to be available."

Hurst said, "Okay, we all must face this. I also want you to get on the phone on my behalf with this list of club owners in other places – find out where there have been any similar incidents before and ask them for any advice they have. It would be nice to assure members that good clubs have survived similar incidents before. Could you also give me a list of extra precautions we are putting in place; however, we communicate that later. And find out when Simon will be back."

"Yes sir."

As Sarto left, Terry Moon, the club's Conditioning Director came into Hurst's office.

"Good morning, Mr. Hurst."

"Terry. Come in."

As Moon sat down, Hurst looked at a big sinewy man. At his interview, Moon had explained to Sarto that he was full Ojibwa. Just after he finished a Bachelor of Science and thinking he might go on to some kind of science doctorate, Moon's two younger brothers committed suicide on their reserve in Northern Ontario. He had then decided to take a degree in something that allowed him to think and apply the rigor of science to the indigenous and any other human body and mind. Dr. Bruce Kidd at the U of T had guided him through that. Moon had qualifications in all the physical disciplines of the well-conditioned human body and several applied psychology credits. He had helped design the club's obstacle course – a very rigorous test of physical and mental skills.

Moon also insisted on giving each of his highest-level clients at Worlds a personal medicine bundle. Mike Keefe had often mentioned Moon as equal to Simon Kiss in his contribution to the excellence of the club.

"Terry, I know Mike Keefe was one of your favorite people. Did you give him a medicine bundle?"

"He was so good he told me the bundle I gave him wasn't quite right for him. He said it should also have burdock. Burdock grew all along the paths through his favorite field as a kid."

"Isn't burdock prickly?"

"You betcha, but it has a lot of medicinal ingredients. He was right about that"

"Have the police talked to you yet about Mr. Keefe?"

"No. But I'm sure they will ask me about his condition."

"Right. So, what will you reply?"

"The man was a very good specimen for a guy his age. No cardio-pulmonary problems on his filed medical record – I watched the good starting heart rate and the efficiency of its rise and fall through a lot of his rigorous workouts, right through to the day he died. He worked out that day around 4:30ish. He said that he'd had too big a lunch."

"Did he confide in you in anything about his life? I mean, I ask you that in case others might ask."

"Yes, he told me several times lately he thought there was something around him going wrong, but he hadn't yet figured out what it was."

"My God, Terry, really?"

"Yes. And I can say that twice lately that I know of he would keep going beyond the end of his rowing – the last exercise in his set, until I inquired, and he thanked me for stopping him. I think he was very preoccupied with something."

"So, sounds like something was seriously bothering him?"

"Yes."

The police cancelled their scheduled 2:00 statement that afternoon. They did not make their next public statement until 11:00 a.m. the following morning, only then saying they could not as yet definitely conclude the primary cause of death was the immediate cardiac failure because the victim had no history of heart problems as evidenced by a recent vigorous stress test he had taken routinely at Toronto General Hospital when he passed the age 60.

Toronto Police's Chief of Detectives, Colin Miservy, said only that tests were continuing on what might have caused the heart failure. He had stone-walled more press questions about why the investigation was continuing. He waved aside a press mob when he and two other detectives slipped past the police line and tapes now surrounding the entirety of World's Club at 11:30 a.m.

At 11:45 a.m. Roy Hurst sat down in the club lounge with three detectives, led by Miservy.

Miservy said bluntly, "Unfortunately we have reason to believe Michael Keefe did not die from natural causes."

Hurst was not quite shocked. "You mean he could have been murdered - possibly from his glass of port?"

"Unfortunately, likely from something he imbibed in the time he was at the club – the port is a possibility we haven't yet ruled out. Because he is such a well-known public figure, we are making double sure, but for all intents and purposes we have commenced a murder investigation. It begins with you, sir, and with Worlds club staff."

Hurst readily replied to the first question as to where he had been at the time of the murder.

"I was not at the club so I cannot testify to any details that night after I left it at 5:30ish to attend a school reunion at Upper Canada College. Many saw me there after 6:30 until after 8:00, as I am sure you will find out. After that I drove to my home in Aurora. Tony Sarto contacted me on my car phone and gave me my first news of Keefe's death at the club."

"What was your involvement with Minister Keefe?"

"Mike Keefe was a founding member of Worlds club. He gained my respect in this period by the way he responded to political allegations of a conflict of interest. Keefe removed himself from having the normal member's small equity interest in the club by donating it to charity and stating that he would never be a member of the club's board or committees."

"That all?"

"Well Keefe stoutly defended his right to retain his basic membership, and his right to play the challenging historical war games in the arcade. "Keeps my strategic brain stimulated," he said. Most leading members of the Governing party and then the front benches of the Opposition Parties have now taken out a club membership.

"What did you discuss with Minister Keefe at lunch?"

"The Minister was very succinct about the issues and the people in his Ministry. His Deputy Minister was an "implementation is everything" veteran of the Ontario Public Service. The Deputy was uncomfortable and simply nodded his head in agreement as Keefe went through the situation."

"And what were you told?"

"The key issue was more than an Ontario investment in computerization of existing business. The issue was should Ontario try to take a leading role in computing advances as such or, as usual, follow the Americans in generic advances? Some key officials, including his senior techie, Martin Davies, were aligned on the side of a big budget-reallocating investment into a new leading edge computing cluster. Most of the Finance bureaucracy are careful soft spoken, "smooth talking," economists. Davies, already known as a "fast talking" techie, was a new boy on the Development side, an American recruited only last year via Ryerson Institute of Technology, down the street."

"My guess is there was resistance to that?"

"You bet. Strong resistance to "risky unknown computer stuff", was their Assistant Deputy Minister, Andy Kinsella, who headed the Industry Division of the Ministry. He's a brush-cut "straight talking" industrial engineer, an advocate of continuing what Ontario business already did well, "leaving it for business to decide the known best use of computers, not Davies' pursuit of known unknowns. Alas, he must have hoisted Davies on his own buzzwords. There was apparently an awful row. But the Minister hadn't even declared his views on the issue yet, so I can't see that as someone's motive."

"To your knowledge, did the Ministry have other business that might have made anyone that angry with Keefe?"

"Well, I can't speak for the whole of the MFD Ministry. But the Local Affairs Division regulates often contentious land use planning and development matters. The Worlds property, which the club leased, was threatened by a competing massive condominium development. I had gone to Cabinet for an anti-condo provincial heritage designation. Apparently, there was as a noisy Cabinet meeting last Wednesday morning on the resulting local Toronto land rezoning issue, taking up more time than the bigger economic and social issues facing Ontario."

"So, anything else about conflict within or about his Ministry?"

"Keefe said the conflict within his Ministry was becoming so serious that the Premier and some senior Cabinet colleagues were already talking of breaking up the super Ministry. The policy issues and personality conflicts were tough ones. Anyway, the conflicting alignments across the Ministry seemed to Keefe to require the kind of organizational development workshop that we at Hurst Associates would be the best suited to help them with."

Miservy said, "So, to sum up, The Ministry was in a state of strong conflict and you were asked to see if you could bring peace by facilitating an executive development workshop. I must ask you, though, might you or the club have had anything to gain or lose by Mr. Keefe's death?"

Hurst gathered his best evasive response to the question.

"Well, that's a sound professional police question getting to motive assuming you are indeed now investigating a murder here. By the way, have the contents of the port glass been found to include a poison?"

Miservy stared silently at him.

"Okay, the answer to your question is the club or I would gain nothing at all from Keefe's death that I am aware of. He was a very active member. In fact, he had drawn many others to take up memberships. We depend in part on some arm's length provincial assistance for the next stage of the strategy gaming in the arcade. Frankly the club could well lose from his death, possibly for quite a while."

"Might that include a loss of the funding you mentioned?"

"It sure might. Who knows what will become of our signature arcade gaming program without Keefe's own huge Ministry supporting it?"

"Right. And did you have any other dealings or relationships with Mr. Keefe, any at all, sir?"

This was beginning to irritate Hurst, but he kept himself under control.

"Nothing. I mean apart from at lunch yesterday agreeing to facilitate an executive workshop. Again, that's something we do often and do well at Hurst Associates."

"Do you have any other relationship? I'm asking that because seemingly irrelevant stuff that people forget comes up inevitably in our investigations. It must be covered. It's best to get it out of the way at the beginning."

Hurst lost his patience.

"Well apart from Keefe being my bastard brother I always hated, and Mother loved far more than me, I can't think of anything…"

Hurst calmed himself.

"Sorry. No, I can think of no other relationship or connection. This has all been a bit much."

The youngest detective was writing this all down excitedly.

Miservy said, "Forget the bastard brother stuff, constable."

The constable looked up in surprise.

"One more question, Mr. Hurst - do you delegate the details of club management to your senior staff? For example, who all would know of the details of the wine and liquor supply?

"I am consulted on a few special purchases. Tony Sarto would be the one to give you those details. Might I ask: if the glass was poisoned, was the whole bottle poisoned?"

"What? Oh, well, we'll be checking into that."

"Do you have the bottle?"

"I think were through for today, Mr. Hurst."

Hurst apologized. "I'm sorry for suggesting anything about your investigation – I advise management in many organizations so that was just my usual curiosity at work. If I do think of anything that might be relevant or come up later, like finding the bottle, I will contact you immediately."

"Thank you, Mr. Hurst."

Part Two:
Late August 1983

Chapter 6

Martin Davies was usually at his office in the Ministry of Finance and Development at 5:30 p.m. He was not, this day. He had left work at 5:00. He was in his condo apartment on Bay Street. It was hard to believe it was already mid-August.

He opened a beer and sat down. His thoughts went back to how he had become involved in matters that had made him pilfer a highly confidential computer tape from his Ministry. The late sun was still shining through the big windows in Davies' west facing Bay Street apartment.

He studied his hands. The nails were immaculately kept, polished like a high society doctor's, nicely shaped, not too big, not too small. They could fly across a computer keyboard. He might have been a medical doctor, a common enough fate for a pharmacist's son. He might have been just about anything he wanted. But he hated the establishment, especially in Philadelphia, to which his otherwise accomplished family had never really been admitted.

It wasn't just their snooty exclusivity that had bothered him about the Philadelphia establishment, as he grew up in West Philly in the late fifties and sixties. It was their complacency.

In the early sixties, it had been about the steady flow of black Americans who moved into his neighborhood in West Philadelphia and were filling up his public school in what had been a mostly working class still white area. School integration was being pushed by some rich Main Line Democrats who would never have thought of living there themselves or sending their kids to a public school even in the white Merion suburbs.

His father, who owned and managed a busy drugstore in West Philly, accepted and lived through that. He stayed there with his family because he believed in fully inclusive democratic values and in serving his neighborhood whoever lived there, regardless of race.

By 1967, there was mounting urban racial anger running both ways. A lot of less advantaged white families felt they had been pushed out of West Philly to live in suburban Delaware County in working class places like Clifton Heights. Some of them were forced to continue to attend for a year or so the now increasingly black schools back where they came from. These whites didn't really have liberal values. The damnable fact was the white families who actually experienced it along the edge of the outward wave of urban racial integration were those whites who were least prepared for it.

Some of those working-class white youth started to come back from Viet Nam, LBJ's other war, to working class suburbs. They were often messed up and limping, some with arms or legs missing - the surviving war-broken, wondering about the ones who would never return. Wondering about who got deferred. Wondering about America, not celebrating their damaged return.

A woman had once come into the drug store needing something late at night when only Martin was there. He recognized her. She had been a babysitter for him. As a kid, he had played with her younger brother, Donny.

"Been a while, huh? How's Donny?"

"Dead - killed in Nam. How much will that cost?"

She didn't even look at him and left.

Davies thought, thank you rich Democrats for your unlived liberal values. But then, he knew that he and many other students at Penn had worked various angles to avoid the draft during the worst Viet Nam war years. Thank you, Martin Davies, yourself, he thought bitterly.

As an undergrad at Penn at the end of the sixties, Davies had only considered two possibilities for his future career: architecture, which he had concluded too often brought you back to the blue bloods, or some latest thing that was moving so fast nobody, even the establishment, could control it yet.

In 1968, halfway through his undergraduate years at the University of Pennsylvania, he had come to realize that the perfect future for him was computers and computerization. He would excel at something that was still new, even in America. Especially in America. He thought it would be a neat indirect way for someone with his math skills to blast away at everything that was wrong with America. Maybe he could help it revolutionize established values and help level the social playing field that way.

Davies had been put right about that by a fellow traveler along the same road he was headed whom he fell in with in his third year. David Sommerfeld was a thin geeky sort of guy, not at all matching Davies' swarthy good looks or up to Davies's work ethic. But Sommerfeld was a guy who came up with enough pithy stuff about the state of America to attract Davies's attention.

"Did you know that one of the guys Ike liked best to play golf with, hated Ike's guts?" "Hey, the rich guy who owns the many of the Ford dealerships in the Midwest was charged twice in New York for insider trading when he was with the finance side of Ford." "Not very many people outside of Hollywood know Cary Grant is gay. I mean Hollywood's top heterosexual star is a homo. Wow!" All sorts of disruptive stuff like that.

The stuff like that had started to add up. And get more pointed. Sommerfeld said to him, "We Americans fool ourselves about how and why we use our power in the world and especially about what's really going on here in America. A few greedy businessmen run the local stuff everywhere and a bigger greedier cartel with their government lobbyists runs the big show!"

"Thank God for unions," Davies had said.

"Hardly touches them. My dad is a union executive. He says, 'we only scrap with them about the last piece of the pie, not the whole pie."

That rang true to Davies as he thought about the hypocritical influence of some of the rich Main Line Democrats on racial integration issues and the new racial mix transforming his part of West Philly and over the endless Viet Nam war. It rang true as he experienced the smugness of many of his wealthy classmates at Wharton and Penn.

Sommerfeld talked an agreeable leftist position inspired by American labor heroes like Joe Hill and the folk and workers' rights music of Woody Guthrie, Pete Seeger, and the Weavers.

Davies and Sommerfeld came from different backgrounds – Sommerfeld's father was indeed a union executive – but they were pleased to discover that they had both gone with their families to join the 1963 jobs march with Martin Luther King and share "the dream" and demand for jobs, rights for the poor and advances on the racial front. It gave them a bond and made Davies more sympathetic to Sommerfeld's stronger socialist ideas.

"The American way is not really the best way, is it?" Sommerfeld had finally challenged Martin one rainy November evening in their last undergraduate year after they had emptied a bottle of bourbon.

"You got a better way? Not the Soviets I hope."

"No. No. I guess I just want to get something better out of America."

"What do you mean? Like hippies? The Yippies. The Weather Underground? Teach at Swarthmore?"

"Well, maybe what's happened is that America needs a much more serious challenge sometime ahead."

"What kind of serious challenge?"

"I don't know yet. Maybe at some perilous future stage of the Cold War - that's at least something Washington gives serious attention to. I've been accepted to lecture in political science and psychology at Northwestern and I'm going to take advantage of their strengths in computer simulation models. That could even lead to a specialty in war simulation gaming. The Department of Defense has approached some of the best grads here at Penn with that next career step."

"So, but do you want to screw up America?"

"No. Wise us up. Especially wise us up to the rich and powerful interests who really run everything. I mean look at most of our classmates. Most of them don't even think about how much dough their parents fork over in Ivy League tuition, and then get a student pass on Viet Nam. I couldn't be here without a huge bursary, and I bet your tuition is a helluva strain on your family.

"Yeah, we own one drugstore in West Philly. Couldn't have done it without a big tuition scholarship. You know Donna Meyer?"

"Yeah, of course – everyone does. She's got it all, including brains."

"Her family owns three big drug stores, both on the Main Line. So, they're probably worth ten times my family. The guy she goes around with, Simon Kiss - his family owned a whole chain of drug stores up in Canada."

"Yeah, I know Simon – he always gets 'A' grades. He's kind of a superior aloof guy. Anyway, to the rich go the spoils, huh?"

"Is it any different or any better anywhere else?"

"Nope."

Davies pressed. "So, why the talk of revolution, man? I mean, here"

"I think we must do better, here, in the States, even if nobody else can. Listen, I went down to Mississippi after my first year and did some civil rights work. Down there it's easy to see how the whole thing is a double bind– even if the blacks gain rights, it's only the rights the whites have and that amounts to a few rich guys and a half dozen companies running everything and the government they influence and pay for its elected bosses fooling everybody else about it. It felt kind of hollow working on just one of the binds. Then I realized that's pretty well the way it is up here too, man. I mean, it's basically a class struggle."

Davies nodded. "Yeah, I was being recruited by Students for a Democratic Society last year and they were like, I should be so excited. And I guess I was, except I realized all they were looking for was talent – not any substantive commitment. I asked the guy about that. He said, well, 'we assume if you're bright enough you'll be committed to the New Left.' Talk about arrogance."

Sommerfeld said, "And I know you're like me and realize this goes deeper. America is in a right-wing mess. Some of us in the know should be working on something better, much better. Something I guess maybe would not look quite like America, as it is now. But a much better future America."

"You're very straightforward with me about this. I mean I could report you on what you just said."

"Yes, but I don't think you will – that would be the Main Line thing to do."

"Well, you're right about that, but most of the rest of America would report you."

Davies nodded. "Anyway, I have told you I'm not any kind of foreign spy on this and I've admitted I don't know what opportunities are ahead. But I bet if, down the line, I came up with something that could help break up America's stupid self-deceptions, you would still be interested."

"You say, 'down the line'. So, you would have to explain it to me then. I can't guarantee I'd go along with it. But I hope my own anger at American self-deception won't have changed."

"Good," Sommerfeld had said.

And then a few days later Davies' anger at America turned stronger.

It was a party – a party where Davies had watched Donna Meyer until he too was besotted by her. He approached her. He had led with an innocent enough comment, "Hi, we're in the same class."

She had replied, "Oh I don't think so, Davies, I am upper, what are you?"

"Well, maybe West Philly to your Upper Merion. But what does that matter?"

She tilted her wine glass at him.

"A lot - I have the means to change the world. You don't. Forget it. Here comes Simon, he has more means than I do. I'll make him a Yippie yet. Thanks, but no thanks."

She had drunkenly wandered over to Kiss and cuddled up to him.

Davies would never forgive her for her insouciant approach to social change as if it were her own plaything. Whatever her social or political views, she was the spoiled rich. He thought there was nothing worse. Overlooking his own brief infatuation, he would also never respect Simon Kiss for falling for her. He had only one thought: 'rich on rich'.

When she was dead two weeks later in a car accident involving some of her stupid Yippie buddies, he heard Simon was broken up about it. He found an early opportunity to try to talk to Simon Kiss about it.

One Friday afternoon he encouraged the emotionally devastated Kiss to accompany a bunch of students who were going over to the "dirty drug," a Penn grad student hangout across Walnut Street.

Davies had never seen anyone so emotionally crushed. Simon simply stared lifelessly at people as they came up to him and expressed their sympathy.

After a while, everybody left them at their booth except David Sommerfeld who came over to give Simon his sympathy and sat down with them. They both were interested to see if Kiss had changed his mind about anything since the accident that had taken Meyer's life. Instead, what little he got from Kiss indicated he may not have much of a mind left.

Sommerfeld took a chance. "Simon, what happened to Donna shows you her way is not the right one."

That had got his attention. "What do you mean?" he seemed irritated at that. At least he was stirring.

"I mean there's no easy way to improve society. I mean Weathermen type of violence. You think?"

Simon said, "The Yippies, now the Weathermen – they messed her up. She had a lot of stupid ideas I didn't sympathize with. But I couldn't reject her thinking out of hand. I guess we argued a lot. She was so willful."

"And so beautiful."

That got more stirring out of Simon. "Yeah. God, I fell in love with her. I didn't mind the anti-war protests. They were peaceful demonstrations, at least if the police didn't go nuts. I couldn't believe she really liked the Yippie guys around her, let alone probably plotted with them on some stupid adventure. I thought she was going to Duke on my suggestion that she should attend an academic conference there."

Simon was now shaking his fists, in anguish.

"I would blow the whole lot of them up if I had a chance to get her back and get her to shape up."

Sommerfeld said, "Well maybe you might help make it right. Here's my number. Just keep in touch and there maybe something you and others can do in the longer run to right a terrible wrong."

Simon had stared at the number on the slip of paper.

"What are you talking about?"

Sommerfeld had repeated the same vague commitment to future social action he had put to Martin Davies. Simon finally put the slip of paper in his pocket and left.

Two nights later, Sommerfeld told Davies that Simon had phoned him and asked, "So what could we do?" They were going to meet the next day, but Simon never showed up.

In fact, neither Davies nor Sommerfeld heard from Simon for several years after that. Simon had apparently borrowed an idea from Sommerfeld, righted himself with an idea for working on the solution to a long-standing problem in game theory and to complete his PhD at Wharton. That eventually led him, through the Rand Corporation, to become the Pentagon's go-to nuclear war games chief.

Martin Davies' immediate hopes of being able to do something interesting with Simon and Sommerfeld had dimmed. Sommerfeld had moved on to his own behavioral specialties, now fully in the Department of Psychology at Northwestern.

Then Davies himself had followed fellowship money to Stanford where he earned a PhD in computer science – one of the first awarded – and allowed himself to be wooed into the private sector by Raymar-Woolrich Electronics in Los Angeles, before taking an assistant professorship at Cal Tech.

There he had done two significant things. He wrote an article for the journal 'Theory and Decision' on conflict resolution decision models that had got the attention of his former friend, Simon Kiss – a call to consider a collaborative article. Before they could agree on that, Davies had been let go at Cal Tech for allegedly plagiarizing the ideas of another professor - a professor known for his right-wing bullying, just as Davies was known for his left-wing ideas.

Davies found out later that the FBI was behind it all. It had also again exposed him to the draft. He had considered conscientious objecting but when he did receive a draft notice, he sought refuge in Canada. It took him several months of impoverished living in 1970s Toronto, at an American draft dodgers' rooming house on Spadina Avenue before his suddenly renewed reputation in 1981 secured the associate professorship at the Ryerson Institute of Technology.

His family had little money left to send him after the forced sale of their drug store in West Philly. By this time, Davies was even more angry at the establishment. Nothing had changed in America. To him, it had got worse.

Chapter 7

Davies realized he would have to go to the police.

The simple fact was that complimentary energy bars had been taped to some of the lockers, including his locker at the central YMCA. and he had offered it to Keefe the next night at Worlds. That probably killed the Minister. His simultaneous realization was that the bar had been intended to kill him and not the Minister. His final realization took only a few moments: the only possible motive to try to kill him was someone whose nose was seriously out of joint because Davies had mailed back to Simon Kiss, the pilfered Rondo tape, instead of giving it to Sommerfeld. Hell, they might even have found out Davies had gone to Keefe the day before confessing his awareness that someone was aggressively trying to obtain the Rondo tape. Keefe had been upset.

Sommerfeld knew these things. Oh shit.

His thoughts went back two years. Davies owed Sommerfeld at least in part for his renewed reputation. The fact was he had never known specifically who "the group" was behind Sommerfeld that got his reputation restored.

At the time, Sommerfeld had contacted Davies in suburban Toronto where Davies was working at a supermarket drugstore. Sommerfeld was visiting Toronto and urged that they meet. Davies readily agreed, thinking maybe Sommerfeld's "sometime down the line project" time had come.

They met at a Deli. Sommerfeld told Davies that he had received an anonymous call from someone who said he knew about both of their career mishaps because of their progressive views. He shared those views and specifically wanted to support strategy gaming as a means to advance the social world. But he shared Davies' own distrust in the best strategy gaming methods so far being only in the hands of Simon Kiss, the man we had known at Penn, whose specialty was now nuclear war gaming in the Pentagon. We agreed Simon was now trapped in a DOD embrace.

"A behind the scenes progressive group with deep pockets," was how Sommerfeld put it. He did not know who headed or worked for the group, which was usually referred to as simply "the group." He said the group thought certain people, especially Davies and I, had been very badly done by in the 70's and wanted to afford us a course of action to recover our careers. In my case, I was hired to edit a popular progressive newsletter and was told my FBI status was improved to a "caution" file."

Davies readily accepted the assistance to restore his own reputation. That had directed his life ever since. Sommerfeld's indirect influence first managed to get Davies included as one of three people in a series of articles in the Los Angeles Times about people being wrongly targeted by the FBI in the late sixties. The sensational series of articles gained back for Davies much of his earlier reputation as a computer whiz kid and someone who had rarely spoken publically against the Viet Nam war despite his public reputation as a moderate leftie. That even brought him an initial offer to return to Cal Tech. But his draft dodging status blocked that.

The group behind Sommerfeld then arranged for some tenured professors here and there to serve as Davies' references for a Ryerson University appointment in Toronto. There, it was further suggested he contact Anatol Rapaport at the U of T, who was then a leading expert in game theory, including using students to run empirical tests of its applications to human conflict.

With that assist and because of his advanced computer strengths, the following year Davies won a competition suggested to him for the position as Executive Director of Technology Innovation in the Ontario Government's Ministry of Finance and Development in Toronto, a powerful department that Davies thought had some progressive tendencies. One of the reasons he thought that was because Simon Kiss, whom Davies had always respected whatever his choice to conduct war games, had been rumored to be headed for Toronto and was part of a grant application to MFD for computer strategy game development out of the new Worlds club.

Sommerfeld knew Davies and Simon had not seen each other in years. He was pleased they had tactfully managed to keep a distance over the months since they had come back into this new contact in Toronto. No one in Toronto knew of their previous student history together.

Sommerfeld anticipated the potential conflict of interest for Davies could result in his being called off the file. The trade-off for career help from Sommerfeld's group was they wanted Davies, for "progressive non-military purposes" to somehow obtain a copy of the Rondo based core tape that was under MFD control in Davies' superior's office.

Sommerfeld had managed to persuade Davies over to the progressive cause in this and he had reluctantly accepted the challenge. He was to keep Sommerfeld posted on his progress in securing the tape.

During the past summer, Sommerfeld himself had again furtively arrived on the scene. There had been several phone conversations with Sommerfeld at local Toronto numbers which he kept changing, urging Davies to continue his quest for the Rondo tape.

To Sommerfeld's satisfaction, Davies forged ahead. No-one seemed to know where the MFD Rondo tape was at MFD until he learned that it was in a lock box high on a shelf in the office of Ted Mathews, his boss, the Assistant Deputy Minister of Technology Development.

One day in early August, when things were sleepy in government departments, Davies went into Mathews' empty office, unguarded for a moment by Mathew's protective secretary. He had a lock pick and picked the lock box and took the tape, concealing it in some newspapers he was carrying and put a blank tape into the lockbox. He had hoped to do duplicate the tape and return the original the next day, with no one the wiser.

But as Davies was closing the lock box, Mathews arrived back at his office. Mathews said, "Martin - glad someone's keeping track of that tape. It's up there on my shelf, and it should have long ago gone down to Legal Services for safekeeping. I keep forgetting to arrange that.

Davies quickly said, "Yes, I just realized that myself. I will do that in the next day or so."

"No need – I'm going down to Legal myself just now." Mathews took the lock box with the now blank tape and headed out of the office. There was nothing Davies could do.

When Sommerfeld next called him at home. Davies explained that he had secured the tape from a box it was in, in a MFD government office and replaced it with an empty tape. But Mathews had taken it to Legal Services. "It likely still won't be realized for a while. But Mathews will recall that I had been putting the box back on his shelf today."

Sommerfeld said, "Okay, Martin. If we've got Kiss' Rondo tape, whatever part of it he just uses at Worlds for the historic war games, you and I have long agreed it can be put to better international uses than just recreational or the real war gaming by the military. He'll probably thank us in the end. You can send it by this courier to this address." He gave a direct delivery address in Topeka, Kansas.

"Right," said Davies, and they hung up.

But then Davies contacted Sommerfeld to tell him he had not sent the pilfered Rondo tape to Kansas because he decided he didn't really know enough about what Sommerfeld's "group" was up to. The whole thing now felt wrong to him. So, instead, he had sent the tape anonymously back to Kiss. He had concluded in a conversation with Sommerfeld, "David, the whole deal with the tape copying is off. I simply can't any longer go along with it. My conscience won't let me."

Sommerfeld had erupted at that. "Well wait, I thought we agreed the conscious part favored doing something better for the world with Kiss' system? You were in full agreement with that. What the hell changed your mind, Martin? I mean you're not the only one out on a limb with this.

"Okay. Okay. I know that. It's just, well it's just anyone I talk to about Kiss thinks doing something better for the world is exactly his own ultimate objective, but that he thinks it will take more preparation and developing a better system. I think he's given as much thought as anyone behind your social science for humanity group, whatever or whoever they are."

"Shit. I guess what you've done is done. I don't know if we should continue our contact."

"No. I suppose not. I wish you well David."

Sommerfeld had hung up. Davies imagined he would dutifully pass on the news to his "group" about the failure with Davies.

On the other side of the broken relationship, Sommerfeld's own intense struggle had begun. How would the group respond to Davies' rogue behavior, or for that matter, to Sommerfeld's failure to "run" him effectively?

After the news of Keefe's death and Davies last call to him admitting that it was Davies himself who had given the "complimentary" energy bar he had received to Keefe and that had likely killed him, Sommerfeld's struggle intensified.

Chapter 8

It was just after 9:00 p.m. Davies was hungry. He had grabbed one or two small sandwiches at the hastily arranged after-hours briefing he had just left at Ontario Hydro headquarters across from Queen's Park on the southwest corner of University Avenue and College Street. The latest projection of Ontario's electricity needs to the turn of the century by those who generated and transmitted it struck him as the usual guessing game, on the demand side usually in excess of what was likely really needed, and on the supply side equally likely well below any realistic cost estimate of the nuclear component. He got off the elevator at the level of the University Avenue subway and took the tunnel to Ontario Government buildings.

The tunnel was slightly curved, the best way to go under the big intersection above and then on to the Finance and Treasury Ministry's Frost Buildings and to the bigger Ontario Government complex another few hundred yards further northeast, which included his own Hurst Block of Ontario MFD Development offices.

By this time of night there were few if any people in the tunnel and he had passed no one, although he was vaguely aware of someone behind him. As he often did, he looked appreciatively at the photos of great Ontario scenes along this part of the tunnel.

As he moved steadily along, it gave Davies time to think through the days since his Minister had been found dead at Worlds. The stark and unavoidable fact was that that night he had given the Minister a poisoned energy bar and he could therefore become the prime suspect. Fortunately, Toronto Police chief of detectives Miservy knew the accidental way Davies had obtained the energy bar and been so far reluctant to arrest Davies.

Miservy had said to Davies after two interviews, "I cannot take you off the suspect list because of the basic fact of how the Minister obtained the poisoned energy bar, namely from you. However, at present I see no motive or pattern that makes me stop at you as the prime suspect. Someone pasted that complimentary bar to your locker, as we know several were taped on several others that day. In fact, this as a warning to you Davies - I think it more likely that you may have been the intended victim and that you unwittingly passed the bar intended to kill you, on to Keefe."

That had shocked Davies. He was reassured that the police at this point felt that no one could have predicted the energy bar would end up with Minister Keefe.

Davies had been thinking hard ever since if there was anyone who would want to kill him. He had the uneasy feeling it must relate to the tape and his connection with Sommerfeld and his group.

Who could be so threatened by that to and to kill someone – him, Davies? He was aware that the gaming at Worlds which was championed by Keefe was an evolution of Simon Kiss' secret military work when he was in the United States. In fact, Kiss had been one of Ontario's big "recruiting back" successes. The idea of simulation gaming had greatly appealed to the policy wonks in the government, of whom he was a leader. But, why murder, likely with himself the intended victim?

Davies started to walk faster in the tunnel. Even so, he heard a person behind him catching up. He wondered if it was someone he knew. He turned to get a look. Just as he was about to speak, the person plunged a knife into Davies' stomach and pushed it around enough to leave him in the tunnel gasping and dying, trying to utter "why?"

Davies was dead before he could finish saying it.

His murderer took Davies' wallet, looked around and headed back to the subway.

Chapter 9

Hurst was fixing himself a whiskey when his phone rang.

"Hello, Mr. Hurst. It's Lyle Lovett, Executive Assistant to the Premier. I'm in the area and I know it's late. I'm wondering of you could possibly spare a few moments for a quick chat?"

Hurst rolled his eyes. "Of course, Lyle. Better than detectives from the Metro Toronto Police. I hope your visit will be a little more relaxed."

He rang off and then called upstairs. He looked at his watch – it was 9:55

Leandra answered. "I invite you upstairs, as usual at his time, when you're not here already."

"That will be good, dear. Alas, it will have to be in a short while. I have another visitor wanting a chat." He explained the delay."

Earlier in the evening, a violent thunderstorm had swept across the north end of the city only briefly relieving the oppressive late August heat wave.

As the sun began to shine again at the busy intersection at the Buttonville general aviation airport, two miles north of the Metro Toronto boundary in Markham, a chauffeured dark blue Provincial Lincoln Town Car just managed to make a left turn in front of on-coming traffic, its wheels whirring on the wet pavement.

Only one of the two back seat occupants seemed to notice the near miss. He was Lyle Lovett, executive assistant to the Premier of Ontario. He smiled tightly and wiped new beads of sweat from his brow, only just dried off from the swelter of the day by the car's air conditioning. Though others tried to ignore it, Lovett had never got used to Jack Charlton's fast driving.

"At this rate Jack, perhaps you should just head out onto the runway and take off. Save us the plane tickets."

Charlton chuckled, "Pilots' union wouldn't allow it, sir."

Lovett glanced at his companion in the back seat, Hugh Bentford. Bentford, a tall man, was coiled up in the corner of the seat still buried in the speech scheduled for the next morning. He was busy highlighting areas for changes to the wording, on the Premier's new instructions, transferred to him by car phone earlier in the drive to the airport, by Lovett, who had the car phone. The speech would then be finalized early the next morning.

As they stopped and Charlton opened the rear doors for them to get out, Lovett closed 5h car phone and said,

"Wait a moment, Jack. I need to change the plans a bit."

"What," muttered Bentford?

"You will have to go on without me. I'll fly up with the Premier tomorrow. She just told me that she needed me to check on another matter."

"Oh, for Christ's sake, Lyle. I was hoping to play pinochle and eat cheezies with you. Now I will be alone in the "flying pencil."" That was the nickname for the long-nosed prop plane based at Buttonville that was reserved for Ontario officials traveling around the province.

"I hope you have a good evening, Lyle."

Bentford was not really upset – he was used to quick changes in plans.

Lovett ducked back into the limo. His chauffeur asked, "Where to now, sir?"

"Jack, do you know where Lesliehurst is?"

"If you mean Roy Hurst's estate on Leslie Street in Aurora, yes. I drove the Premier and Mike Keefe to a dinner party there recently. We should make it in about twenty minutes."

"Good. Let's go. I just called him on the car phone. I will only be there a short while and then you can drive me back downtown. I'll need to see the Premier."

"Okay. Got it."

As they headed north again, Lovett could see the flying pencil take off from the airport and pass overhead.

Roy Hurst waited in the library as the big old Niagara-built clock chimed seven times. "Something of particular concern to the Premier" was how Lovett had explained his request to drop by for a chat.

He to the French doors and looked out at the hills. Sometimes that view could absorb all his cares. Outside was still steaming after the storm and Hurst was beginning to steam as well. Too many interruptions these days.

It was a long list. He knew the consultancy was overcommitted and, late the previous day, Hurst Associates had lost an important corporate client for that reason. That would not have happened if he hadn't held back some scarce resources for what often turned out to be and, in this case, turned out to be unpredictable off-and-on government work. Well, he supposed he couldn't blame the government for Keefe's death at Worlds. That had thrown the club into turmoil and closed it for three days. Then Simon disappeared. The police had already interviewed Hurst three times. And now it sounded like the Premier had sent Les Lovett up for a "chat," once more intruding on him and Leandra.

Hurst managed to regain some composure with some mental exercises Leandra had taught him. He had just turned back into the library when he heard the distant door chime.

Leandra herself brought Lovett to the library. Though she too was troubled by Lovett's visit, she smiled brilliantly at her husband and left the man at the door for her husband to welcome.

"I must seem very ordinary looking beside your lovely wife," said Lovett.

"Maybe a bit crumpled. That's understandable after a long hot day and the rain perhaps," chuckled Hurst.

"You are most kind."

"May I offer you a drink?"

"Scotch rocks would be perfect."

They sat down.

"To what do I owe this sudden visit?"

"I appreciate you seeing me with little notice, Mr. Hurst."

"Understood Les and I have asked you before to call me Roy."

"If you don't mind, I still prefer to refer to important people in this Province as Mr., Dr. or whatever or if ladies, Miss, Mrs., Dr., Ms. or whatever these days. Compared to them I am but a minion."

"Some minion! Well, maybe a filet. But okay, Les, what's up?"

"Well, in confidence, the Premier herself had recently begun to worry about the Ministry of Finance and Development. It had started marvelously with Mike Keefe's firm hand, but the Minister himself was beginning to feel that the conflict level was getting too high in the Ministry, even for him."

Nothing new yet, Hurst thought.

"As a matter of fact, he called the Premier in the late afternoon of his last day saying that he had had a talk with you about it at lunch and that you would be available for an executive conflict management workshop to be in the next few days."

"Yes, that was what we agreed to."

"Minister Keefe also indicated to the Premier that an additional problem had just come to his attention. It was arranged that the Premier and I would meet with him early the next morning to discuss the new problem whatever it was. That was at 5:00 p.m. that day. Both the Premier and I had to leave for a function right after that and we weren't an easy contact for the rest of that night."

Lovett accepted a refill of his scotch rocks.

"Since then, we've all been in a state of shock over Keefe's death. I've had a few brief conversations with the Premier about it. At first, she was hoping the arrangement you had made with Keefe could be carried out and that the MFD could be kept together. Then yesterday she did an about-face on that. She told me she thought MFD would have to be broken up as soon as possible."

"Well Lyle, you know better than me that political priorities can rapidly change."

"Yes, but this was the first time on anything that big she did it without my knowledge. It was very sudden. I sort of wondered about it."

"I see."

"On the drive up to the airport today I was finally getting around to a backlog of phone messages. To my chagrin, there were no less than three attempts later that evening by Keefe to get a hold of the Premier or me. The last message left it that he would have to hit us cold at our meeting the next morning with whatever was bothering him. If only he had been able to reach the Premier or me things might have been different."

"So, whatever was developing through late last Tuesday was increasingly upsetting him. And he couldn't contact anyone at the top to share it."

"Exactly. So, seeing Keefe's urgent efforts to contact us, I'm wondering was there anything in your conversation at lunch that day that suggested what was developing through the day that came to upset him so much later in the day?"

"Nope. We were only discussing the need for an executive workshop. The whole lunch was fairly relaxed."

"I hate to press, but are you sure that was all he mentioned?"

Somehow that kicked up something Hurst had forgotten.

"Now that you mention it, when he first sat down, and his Deputy was approaching, he said he wanted to talk just to me about something. But that got lost in the rest of the lunch."

"Well, something was sure bothering him. If only he had been able to reach the Premier or me, things might have been different."

"You're not the only ones. Keefe also called me, later that night, actually just a few minutes before his death, with the same kind of message he left with you."

"I am going to ask you what I fear you may understandably resist: once more to summarize what you discussed with the Hon. Keefe at lunch that day."

"Well, you've got the "once more" right. I'm a little fed up with doing that, but I have never done it for the Premier's office, so here goes." Hurst gave a succinct version of what Keefe had discussed with him and his commitment to do an executive workshop a few days later.

"Thank you. I had to check to make sure there was nothing the Premier and I did not know. So, you're sure Keefe didn't mention any issues at the MFD other than the turf spats resulting from his decision to put a big new strategic economic emphasis for Ontario on basic computer innovation?"

"The police keep asking me that. No, nothing else – I gather that a computer science initiative, as such, was his policy preference over basically just going along with a follow-the-Americans computer take-up by our established industries and business clusters."

"It doesn't sound that the Deputy Minister was an active participant in your conversation at lunch."

"No, I would say most decidedly not."

"Thank you, Mr. Hurst. That is what we had to know."

"Do I get a clue about what this may tell you? After all, you are here because I am as they say, a 'friend of the government'."

"Not yet, and perhaps it doesn't lead anywhere. It probably rules out anything obvious tying together Worlds and MFD if the Deputy was unaware of it. His lassitude you describe at lunch does not suggest he was alarmed about anything. Mind you, there was quite a lot going on in that Ministry. Some of it obviously had set off battles about the province's overall economic emphasis. If there is a smoking gun, I hope it will have nothing directly to do with Worlds. The Premier wanted me to tell you that. You will be one of the first outside of government and the police to be informed if it was a government issue that someone tried to resolve in your club. I shall see to that. Thank you very much for your time, Mr. Hurst."

Hurst wondered if even clever politics could save the club. He simply shook his head, then shook Lovett's hand and escorted him to the front door.

As he did, Leandra came hurrying up to the men. She was looking stressed.

"I'm sorry to interrupt. Lovett, but there is news just now on TV that an MFD Executive Director named Martin Davies was just found murdered at Queens Park."

Lovett took this news with difficulty and leaned against the front door. "Oh my god. Davies was such a talent. Sometimes things just get too hard." He kept shaking his head.

"Please come back to sit down before you leave, Les," said Hurst.

"Thank you but no. The Premier will need me more than ever now."

"Give her our support then."

"Yes, I will. Good evening, Roy."

"Good evening, Lyle."

Hurst guided him out through the front door.

He drew Leandra to him, and they walked together back to the library.

"Roy, what in heaven's name is going on?" she said to him.

"I haven't the faintest idea."

Chapter 10

Karl Maddow picked at an omelet as a late August morning sun poured through the window of the study in his home in the countryside beyond Houston. He closed the newspaper he was reading and tossed it aside.

The small article he had just read in the inner pages was headlined "Second most Senior Official in Ontario Government Dead under Mysterious Circumstances."

He didn't need reminding things had gone badly wrong in Toronto.

The fact was things had too often gone wrong in his life. He was born in a small town in Texas. He had moved with his family around and up to Austin, the State capital, as his dad had become a top lobbyist for the oil business. As a big kid, he was expected to be the strong silent type. To be an athlete. He was neither. He liked science and math at school and didn't seem outwardly to care much about what other kids and people said about him. And every time he spoke up about something, everybody thought he was "a problem." His parents never took his side. He knew they always blamed him for not being a strong silent athletic type.

Even so, Maddow had been sent to "the best" schools. He had ended up at the University of Pennsylvania where he got caught up in a John Birch Society demonstration. He was famously caught in a news photo carrying a sign with a mistaken 'a" reading "Break the Bank!" among other signs reading "Break the Bunk", alluding to a local Bircher's statement that allegations against the Society were socialist "bunk." His family was fed up with his careless activity and cut him off. In the next few years, Maddow had had to scramble to get his way to a degree by becoming adept at computer programming and a go-to problem-solver at various computer labs and centres around Philadelphia. He returned to Texas where he became a key advisor to the oil industry. He had become rich and had made some much richer and powerful Texan friends in the oil patch. Two of those guys had met with him several years back and convinced him to turn his computer skills to simulations of consumer preferences and public opinion responses to various oil industry public relations strategies.

His mind drifted forward to the phone call that had triggered the Toronto situation. A call that could connect him to the events in Toronto but had given him no choice. He had gotten so close to Rondo. Or at least the part of it he needed that was worth so much to him. How it weighed and scored gaming outcomes for their realism based on the underlying social-psychology of the teams.

But one of the operatives Maddow had so carefully planted in Toronto context had turned on his plot -he had stolen the Rondo tape and then sent it back to Kiss! Maddow had to come up with a plan, and quickly. He smiled inwardly that he had for a while had contingency plans for turned operatives – two in D.C., two in California, and his two in Toronto – Davies and Sommerfeld. He activated the plan for Davies – a "complimentary" energy bar, insidiously poisoned with aconite which would feign a natural death, a bar that Davies would surely use while jogging. It would be placed in Davies' locker at the new Toronto central YMCA by a skilled hit man Maddow also had retained for possible Toronto assignments.

Maddow had also hoped the whole thing would not only take out Martin Davies, but also expose Simon Kiss on suspicion of murder – after all, Davies had stolen his precious RONDO core tape.

People who got in his way. People he didn't like, who were stupidly idealistic to the left. They made him very angry. People like Martin Davies who could expose him. People like David Sommerfeld, who Maddow had so carefully selected to run Davies.

The first thing that went wrong was the events he arranged for had happened when Kiss was not in Toronto because of last-minute flight changes leaving him in Montreal for several days. His brilliant "perfect murder" plan had proceeded without a fail-safe – no-one could get through to delay the hit guy in time to stop the first death. And so, the first death via the ingenious complimentary energy bar was the wrong man.

The wrong man was alas a very important government guy whose death was causing great publicity and intense investigations up there. That might also mean there would now have to be another murder – of the intended victim. Yet would that not bring all kinds of new intense enquiries.

His immediate concern was now both Martin Davies and David Sommerfeld could lead to him. Sommerfeld was the partly unwitting accomplice between Martin Davies and the phony organization Maddow had set up to attract Sommerfeld: Citizens for Progressive Social Science, whose vague mission was "Social Science Helps the World!" Sommerfeld had fallen for it, hook, line, and sinker. But if he was already seriously wondering about Keefe's death, and he certainly would be distraught if his friend Davies was also killed in "the group's" interest.

So, did that in turn mean Maddow would need to get rid of Sommerfeld too? Sure, the guy had repeatedly professed his continued loyalty. Certainly, he had been a surprisingly gullible idealist. But he was too smart not to realize he had likely been duped because of his bleeding-heart socialism. Certainly, unlike any take-out of Davies, offing Sommerfeld, someone unknown to the public and with no high status, might not add much to the public excitement up there. But Sommerfeld, unlike Davies, could be directly traced back to Maddow.

Maddow could not yet decide what further action in either Davies or Sommerfeld's case might be now necessary in Toronto. He had already ordered a delay.

He was inwardly cursing the situation when his phone rang.

"What?"

He listened for a moment.

"WHAT," he now exclaimed! Your last instructions were to wait. Get the hell out of Canada, now!"

He slammed down the phone and began to pace the room. "Why must events I drive end up driving me? Why? Why?" he kept muttering.

Part Three:
September 1983

Chapter 11

Simon's fellow senior techie at the Pentagon between 1979 and 1983 was Leslie Lipson.

On the Friday evening of the Labor Day weekend in early September, Lipson was sitting in a leather seated booth at the Red Goat Inn, a secluded hostelry in Virginia about sixty miles southwest of Washington.

Hidden by thick yew hedges, the entrance to the Red Goat was regaled with a bronze fountain featuring a revolutionary "skirmisher" and a mascot goat. In local fable, the goat escaped, covered in his master's blood, during a local disagreement between Royalists and "the Patriots" in the 1776 revolutionary war.

The Inn was the only commercial establishment in a mid-Virginia crossroads hamlet known locally as Red Goat Corners. The Red Goat was the least known of a network of Virginia inns used by the military for off-site meetings and workshops. It functioned well for those high-ups in the know wanting to have a quiet off-the-record-meet.

The Inn's interior decor was red and black. Lipson was noticing the reds as he sipped a surprisingly good local Virginia wine. He was waiting to be joined by a couple of three-star generals. There wouldn't be introductions – he had reported to them almost daily since he had helped Simon Kiss develop the Rondo strategic nuclear war gaming system for the Pentagon in 1980.

Lipson had a doctorate in political science from Southern Illinois University, where he had caught the computer simulation fever going through the "hard" social science community in the early 1970's. He and Simon Kiss had met when both were doing a stint at the Rand Corporation in Los Angeles a few years later.

Lipson recalled that Simon had come into social simulation from the truly "hard science" mathematical game theory side. Simon was a follower of Anatol Rapoport and was trying to apply the mathematics and logic of game theory to a social-psychologically tested human-computer gaming platform for actual games played. His approach tested hypotheses about actual human behavior in strategic decision making, for which he had quickly earned his doctoral degree from the University of Pennsylvania. In fact, Simon's doctoral dissertation was so innovative and so sensitive that the military, who had in part paid for it, decided it should be withheld from publication.

Both Simon and Lipson had then done good work for the Rand Corporation, before the military decided they could reel them in and employ them directly with more security and at lower cost. Both men were brought into the DOD in 1979.

Lipson now marveled at how Simon had somehow recently managed to "escape" the Pentagon, though he was not unloosed from the Pentagon's "extreme security risk" hook.

The two generals arrived. They brought their drinks from the bar and sat down in Lipson's booth, one opposite him and the other pressing Lipson into the corner on his side. Both men were very large Generals, one army, one air force. Unlike the slight and civilian suited Lipson, who had red hair that included a neatly trimmed goatee, they were cleanly shaven to emphasize their strong jutting chins.

Lipson had faced them the day before in a small room in an isolated corner of the Pentagon. At that meeting, the generals had put Lipson on notice to "explain to us what was going wrong in the nuclear gaming room" and be able to do so to their satisfaction at the Red Goat, the very next evening at 7:00 sharp.

So, now it was 7:20 p.m. This was it.

One of the generals was Lamont Walker, a native of Bland, Virginia. He was known as "Big" Walker not just for his own size but for the famous Big Walker Mountain near his birthplace. Walker was also big as the top military advisor to the Intelligence Advisory Committee of the Joint Chiefs of Staff. His equally large buddy was General Norman Thalemann, a former all-star Cornhusker left tackle from Nebraska and the Air Force general in operational command of nuclear forces. He was the other top military advisor to the Intelligence Advisory Committee. The two hulking men were similar in appearance, except that Walker had a full brush cut and Thaleman had only thinning hair left on his head.

Walker leaned forward and looked at Lipson.

"We meet at last. Red Goat's the right place for you – I mean you got a red goatee!"

The generals laughed until Thaleman had a fit of coughing.

Walker continued, "So, Lippy, you figured out a way to stop that damn computer flashing red in the Love Nest?"

Walker had figured in 1980 that 'Lover' should be the code name for a back-channel game designed to maintain a MAD nuclear embrace with the Soviets. The gaming room for it in the Pentagon was called the 'Love Nest'. After all, the gaming platform was invented by a guy named Kiss.

Lipson smiled. "Ah well, it does sometimes seem a mischievous 'Lover.' Indeed, your own ingenious code name for it, Big."

Walker didn't even nod at that. He just continued, "I mean if you scientists have your doomsday clock always near midnight, we military guys have our own balance scale. It should always be tilted just a bit our way. That way, we continue to ensure mutually assured destruction. That's one helluva result we strategic military achieved on our side and then with the Soviets."

Lipson shook his head. "The clock belongs to the nuclear scientists – I am not one of them. Simon and I are game theorists and behavioral political scientists, trying to apply our knowledge of actual human behavior to your rarified strategic nuclear war gaming, although, I admit we both think it is absurd for anyone to have, let alone game, the means to blow up the planet."

"Okay, so you guys didn't build the big doobies. Just put us generals on a strong leash. But, damn it, we've just gone from a flashing orange alert on that computer in the Love Nest to a red light alert. I had to shush you from telling us why yesterday. Too many people around. I want to tell you, it's eerie being in that war gaming room with the red light flashing. Thalie here and I want it stopped."

Thaleman nodded." You've got that right, Big."

Lipson shrugged. "Well, that was Simon's idea. I was about to tell you that Simon's current analysis of news and intellig3nce apparently led him to anticipate a bunch of counter measures the Soviets could use to respond to President Reagan's just announced commitment to a full-out strategic ABM defense. Anyway, I warned you last week, Simon could remotely 5un on the flasher."

"I'm the guy to issue warnings, not you," said Walker.

Lipson shrugged again. "When that warning occurred in the Love Nest it's because Simon's own analysis shows the Soviets can much more readily deploy new offensive counter measures to counter the ABM shield we're pissing around with, than we will be able to build anti-countermeasures shield to defeat their ABM defeating measures. Simon told you: Anti-Anti-Anti doesn't stabilize."

Thaleman crunched on a steak bone and said, "I don't understand why. Shouldn't ~~Three~~-three antis maintain another kind of strategic nuclear balance: neither side knows what will get through? Plus," he winked at Walker, "We would have the advantage."

"MAD is a stable solution only if both sides know unacceptably vast damage to each side occurs even after a first strike by either side. Anything like us thinking we have deployed a full ABM would be God knows what - shaky, shaky. You better get used to the red light – it's a signal from Simon that we are in a real destabilization period."

The Generals ordered more drinks.

Lipson pressed his temporary advantage. "Anyway, this shouldn't be a surprise. In 1980, neither side gamed out of MAD. Now our own decision-makers have broken that symmetry. In fact, Simon's fear of our departure from MAD with a destabilizing ABM defense initiative was a big reason he left. Our side has started to take a complete ABM defense seriously because of a new President and his silly Star Wars talk that has gone beyond our 1980 gaming. As Simon feared."

Walker nodded and took a call on a phone brought to him. Thaleman munched and remained silent.

Walker rang off. Whatever it was made him look again at Lipson in disgust.

"That was General Edmonds. I asked him to check. He says the guys who would play our nuclear gaming simulation this time around don't agree with the behavioral testing and assumptions Simon forced on them in 1980."

"Well, they agreed to take the psychological tests. They weren't forced to do so. We analyzed the results and weighted gaming results accordingly and accurately as to the prospects for continued MAD stabilization. They have no expertise to bring to bear. That's part of Lover. I suggest they end their little rebellion. Full stop!"

"Okay, I figured you and Kiss would take that position. So then, we need a new 'kiss'. Our people agree that the Reagan Administration and the Soviet bunch under Andropov are different than the last bunch – everything will have to be done again – we need a new back game."

Lipson replied, "Simon tells me he's heard that the Soviets are now more genuinely afraid of a nuclear war than in 1980. That's their predictable reaction to our rapid emplacement of intermediate ICBMs in Europe to match their own SS missile emplacements. We did that a lot faster than they thought we would."

"Okay, how about that false alarm the occurred about incoming American ICBMs over there?"

"Now that was scarier, and we think more interesting. When I last talked to Simon, we agreed that was done to unsettle us enough to consider some new talks. I think that followed both our rapid intermediate missile emplacements and President Reagan's announcement of an all-out strategic missile defense initiative. I think they see Reagan's aggressive writing on the wall. Simon and I think they now might try some even bigger strategic distractions and we had better be ready for that. The Korean airliner shot down the other day may be just the beginning."

Lipson was referring to Korean Air Lines Flight 007 a scheduled Korean Air Lines flight from New York City to Seoul, via Anchorage. On September 1, 1983, the airliner was shot down by a Soviet SU-15 interceptor in the Sea of Japan. All passengers and crew aboard were killed, including Lawrence McDonald, a sitting member of the United States Congress. The civil aircraft was alleged by the Soviets to have flown through prohibited Soviet airspace around the time a U.S. reconnaissance mission had done the same thing.

The two generals welcomed the cheesecake desert.

Walker said, "So you think this is all an alert about dangerous distractions, but not yet the real thing?"

"Well yes, and you better be ready for more. What about a nuclear accident on one of their subs, say, a hundred miles off Long Island?"

"You really think they could distract us from deploying an ABM defense with random nuclear side-events to distract us?"

"Not just us – our own public opinion and our very jittery allies too. That's why there's that alarm in the gaming rooms."

"Okay maybe we need to validate that. So, like I said, we need a new kiss. Simon declined when we discussed it last December. Can you do it without Kiss?"

This was the question Lipson was waiting for.

"No, I would need Simon. Only he could stop the flashing red light."

"Wait a minute, I can pull the fucking plug on them any time we want," said Thaleman.

"Not so easy – they're part of Kiss' whole system, you know. Who knows – we might lose the whole thing."

"What the fuck. You mean he put in a trip wire or something."

"Sort of, I think."

Walker was sizzling.

Thaleman said, "Lamont, can't we call Simon back any time we want, isn't that the deal with him?"

Lipson interceded. "Yes, but not necessarily get his help any more than he is providing at the Worlds Club in Toronto."

"What help?" asked Thaleman.

"Well damn it, you're in the loop. He's still validating the Rondo approach to strategic behavior. It could be a huge solution in social science, and not just for the military. His theoretical conjecture that a dynamic strategy game tends either to permanently stabilize or permanently destabilize without learned cooperation after six definable moves based on his two key intersecting behavioral curves might even be the first mathematical constant in social science. Well maybe after six degrees of separation relating every human."

Lipson looked directly at the generals. "It's all in his 1972 article in the "Theory and Decision" journal your military bosses continue to suppress. Much of the seemingly innocuous recreation gaming he is doing in Toronto is a quasi-experimental trial testing of his theoretical behavior-based strategy gaming models."

Walker stared back at Lipson. "All well and good. Anyway, Thalie and I want Kiss back – at least for a while."

Lipson said, "He might resist."

"So what?" said General Thaleman, looking at Walker, who nodded in agreement.

"We'll just bring him in. You should be there."

Lipson said. "Okay, but I don't think you'll get much from him at this point. Also, doesn't the CIA have an interest? It's outside the U.S."

"Well, it will have to be a joint exercise."

"You think?" said Thaleman.

"Simon doesn't take well to interrogation," said Lipson.

"The strawberry cheesecake was good," said Walker.

Chapter 12

"For Christ's sake, you're going to blow my cover in Toronto."

Simon had not been that surprised at being kidnapped – the Pentagon was obviously wondering what the hell was going on in Toronto and wanted to know immediately, even if it was awkward to yank Simon out. But the personal fall-out for Simon alone still made him angry.

The driver said, "Well, not us guys. Maybe whoever we report to, and they report to is. We just make the deliveries. The order said pick up and deliver one Dr. Simon Kiss – ASAP, no trace numbers."

"But a good friend of mine is expecting me tonight. Do you - do they expect my Toronto contacts to just shut up?"

"Not for us to know or decide. We just take you to Mount Hope airport in Hamilton and off you go."

Simon knew his protests were useless and he couldn't say anymore without endangering the Hursts.

The flight on a Lear jet from Hamilton lasted a little over an hour before getting around to landing in a remote part of Baltimore-Washington International airport. Simon was surprised – he thought it would go to Andrews AFB if his destination was the Pentagon or the CIA.

Kiss was piled into a van and driven for another three quarters of an hour to Annapolis Maryland. He was led into a small hotel just down from the clock tower and told to order anything he needed from room service, including toiletries and fresh clothes.

"Wish we could do that for you, but that's not our job. Bye now."

Simon had said nothing more to his deliverers.

He was exhausted and after ordering for the next morning, sacked out immediately. He awoke at 5:30 in the morning, started receiving a bunch of delivered stuff, showered, put on fresh new clothes, accepted a full room service breakfast and newspapers and decided it was sort of his lot in life.

Except: what would Sabina think? She was too smart, too actively inquisitive, too concerned about Simon to leave it alone. Damn it he cursed inwardly – I know I should not love her, but I can't help loving her. It's essential to me now. They'll never get that out of me.

At 7:30 he got a call to come to the small conference room on the second floor for an 8:00 meeting.

He walked into the room at 8:10.

Everybody in the room except Les Lipson, to whom he nodded a greeting, was pissed off at Simon's casual lateness.

The rest sitting around a big oval board table included the only two three-star generals he knew well and a couple of suits he hadn't seen before whom he concluded were CIA.

Simon said, "My favorite thing – an interrogation."

General Walker leaned toward him and growled, "You better hope you get through it."

It wasn't the growly generals who concerned Kiss. They were, after all, mostly on his side. It was the CIA interrogators. They would know how to pry, and they would pry.

They introduced themselves as Ben Sturgess and Bill Warrington, leaving it to General Walker to add "These men are experienced CIA interrogators. Ben and Bill are known as the "Killer B's. You better be up to their stings."

Sturgess was as big as the generals. Like Walker, he had a brush cut. He wore black-rimmed thick-lensed glasses that exaggerated his look at anyone. Warrington was an Afro-American of average size who gave Simon a pleasant smile. Simon did not need to wonder much who was the good cop and who was the bad cop.

"Well, go to hell all of you. But before that, let's get this over with."

Warrington chuckled.

The good cop, for sure, Simon thought.

Sturgess led with some hard stuff, glaring at Simon like a bird of prey.

"Dr. Kiss, let's review some current events - do you know what's really going on at your club up north? You see, the problem we must get at here, is that Toronto was supposed to be a quiet site for your further development of the war gaming. Now it might as well be Hollywood central for the Cold War."

"That would be 'Hollywood North'.

"Either way, it seems a much more active place than we thought, from an intelligence viewpoint. But maybe you fooled us on that. I'm going to read you what you said before that decision to let you go to Toronto was made."

"I am a native Torontonian. It's a polite place, maybe in some ways still a bit of a backwater, but its great university has a good big IBM computer, as big as at Michigan or MIT and lots of scope to continue the psychological testing of the Rondo program without unnecessary snooping. It also has a new mid-town club where I can behaviorally validate some of our gaming using unsuspecting members who are mostly, in their own worlds, strategic decision-makers."

Sturgess put down the document. "Some intelligence backwater. It's a commie flee bed, isn't it?"

"Well, there are indeed some commies there, like anywhere else outside the United States and even here in a few places. I don't think we've had any problem that way."

"You mean with your set-up in Toronto?"

"Yes."

"I'm sure you know that Anatol Rapoport is at the U of T."

"So?"

"He's a commie sympathizer He left the U.S. because he opposed the war in Viet Nam."

"Okay, he is there. We follow each other's work. So far as I know, he's not a commie. I suppose for you guys, leaving the States in opposition to the Nam war constitutes being a commie?"

Warrington said in a friendlier tone, "Did you know that he's all over your computer work at the U of T."

"In what way?" That bothered Simon.

"The university computer room routinely was giving him copies of what you're doing. We found that out and stopped it. It was hushed up of course."

"Well, you hushed it up even from me. If they do or did, I was not aware of it. Does the University of Toronto computer room work for Rapaport?"

"No. Not directly. But he still has a faculty cross-appointment there and he fooled the computer room people into thinking you were permitted to use the university computer because he was one of your research collaborators. He said it should be an informal arrangement because you didn't want to make other faculty members demand the amount of computer capacity you sometimes use. Tricky guy, huh?"

Rapoport was one of Simon's heroes. Did Rapoport really do all this? Simon thought he would like to find out.

"We were told that Rapoport is quite ingenious in finding out about the latest work that is related to his own. But we don't think he was involved with the Worlds side. He wasn't a member, nor did anyone take him there as a guest – his photo was not recognized by any of the staff, including the one you call the porter, who seems to have a photographic memory of all who come and go there."

"Well Powell is very reliable that way, and after all, he is one of the operatives you and the Mounties have placed there."

Only Lipson was a bit surprised.

Simon said, "So, why am I here?"

Sturgess took that question. "It seems clear that someone was trying to access your Rondo program the night the guy," he checked his notes, "that very important guy Keefe was killed."

"Yes, the full nature of the shut-down would indicate that. Whether it was connected in any way to Keefe's death remains unclear."

Warrington said, "Perhaps we can initially leave that to the Toronto police investigation."

"They are doing a very thorough investigation," confirmed Simon.

Warrington continued, "But Simon, this gives us a reason to get to any other possible interest in your work over the years. We want to review the past. Let's go back to when you and Lipson worked at the Rand. That was four to six years ago. Who knew about your work there?"

"No one there but the top two business partners, and they had little or no idea technically what it was about. It was just a conveniently placed piece of DOD contract work."

Sturgess leaned forward. "What about the article you were going to publish in that journal…' He checked his notes, in 'Theory and Decision'?"

"Well, DOD had already put me on notice about that. I was just leaving Penn. In fact, the Mathematics Trust which knew about the article was upset because they had largely funded my graduate years at Penn, and I had submitted the first version of the article while I was still a grad student. When I was about to send them a copy, I was paid a little visit by the Dean of Graduate Studies at Penn who persuaded me not to. My reversal of an earlier agreement to share a copy upset some of the Trust people. I had to tell their lawyer to contact another lawyer whose name the Dean had given me who would quietly lay out the national security sensitivity of the article."

Sturgess wasn't about to give up. "We understand that you also had a mental break-down in your last year at Penn."

"Yes. That's probably what it was. I guess I was working too hard. It all mounted up. Quite a few intense students experience something like that."

"That, plus a girl friend of yours, Donna Meyer was killed in a car accident. Isn't that true?"

Uh oh, thought Simon, they're getting to my first line of defense.

"Yes. She and I had become good friends and I felt guilty that I had encouraged her to go to a math and physics conference at Duke University. I didn't realize she also wanted to help agitate against the war down at Duke. It's still hard for me to believe - she went down with some crazy Yippies, one of whom was Weathermen Underground. It was never clear how the accident occurred. It was a bad time, especially for her, huh?"

"Yes. We heard that another crisis for you at that time was criticism from a fellow student," said Sturgess.

"Geez. I don't think anything like that caused a crisis for me."

"So, what happened – why are we misinformed?"

"Maybe you mean the big Political Science department party I attended when I was doing my doctorate. Boy you're good – how'd you dig that up? Anyway, yeah, that was the time a guy went on about 'some' students who had never experienced a real challenge before in their work and were prematurely judged and favored as the most promising. He called such favored students, 'swishers', like basketball players good at sinking long shots. Donna told me that the guy was just jealous of me. I hadn't even realized he was referring to me - that was how naive I was at the time."

Warrington said, "Well, Simon, that same David Sommerfeld went on to become the Executive Director of the Mathematics Trust, didn't he?"

Simon thought, oh, oh, there goes my second line of defense.

"Yes, he did join the MT. And I guess it's true I learned he had a copy of my unpublished journal article, and he led their battle in trying to publish it or at least retain ownership of it."

"And you never had any other contact with him?"

"One or two meetings and then a few phone calls over the years. Something about working on progressive things – a peace project or something. Nothing that I can recall in any detail."

Simon was being deliberately evasive – the questioning was getting to one of Simon's curses. His last line of defense. The fact was that he truly couldn't remember what was discussed in the calls after Penn with Sommerfeld. It was a blank.

Sturgess said, "That guy is on our list and the FBI list for his so-called "peace" activities and attempts to recruit others. Why the hell would a dedicated peacenik keep in touch with a guy who does war games?"

"I've said many times, gaming war is not waging it, especially if you are trying to prevent it. He was likely attracted to that side of me. But I can't remember what we discussed. Surely nothing important if my memory is so vague."

"Well, try to recall more and if you do, we want to know."

Then he changed the subject.

"Okay. Now let's move to you, General Walker."

Walker turned on Warrington. "What the hell do you mean - I'm not the subject of this interrogation for Christ's sake."

"As it happens, yes, you are, or at least one the subjects. Tell us about your membership on the Board of the Mathematics Trust. Were you not recently a member of that select group from 1974 to 1982?"

Chapter 13

Walker opened the cellophane on a cigar, chewed the end, spit it into the big ashtray beside him on the table and spent some time lighting it.

"Yeah. I guess. Both my parents sort of ran it. They were wealthy people who thought pure math and science would strengthen America and donated a few million bucks to help. That got them the board memberships. Then Dad died and Mom insisted that I replace him. So what?"

Sturgess' magnified eyes stared at him. "Just this – here's a guy Kiss knows, who is maybe a heavily committed leftist radical, maybe even a commie, and you're on the guy's board of governors through a critical time in the development of Simon's strategic war-game work."

Walker puffed on his cigar.

"Well, that jerk Sommerfeld sure thought it was 'his' board. He was a young know-it-all asshole. Mother told me she regretted having approved of him as the Executive Director. The little bastard tried to get stuff through us like we were rank amateurs. But that was after the time MT gave funding support to Simon Kiss' doctoral work."

Sturgess said, "So now that we know you and Kiss both share some background with the Mathematics Trust, let's see if we can piece together any interconnections. Let's keep going with you General Walker. When did you attend any board meetings at MT in, let's say, 1980?"

"Oh for Christ's sake. I usually did them by phone if they needed a quorum, but I guess I did attend one or two."

Sturgess pressed, "Was it one or was it two?"

Walker scowled. "Two, I guess. I'd go up if there was some good reason. They had their board meetings on Fridays, so you could make a long weekend of it. I went up there in March because one of the few people I liked on the board, a retired math and physics teacher from West Point, had tickets for a Flyers hockey game. Those guys play rough – we could have used them in Nam. In fact, as I recall that Thursday was St Patrick's Day - lots of green in Philly."

"March 17th."

"Yeah. I guess. The other time was sometime in the fall, I think the week of Halloween. Yes, it was Halloween on the Monday because we drove home that day. Thaleman, you should remember that. We went up with our wives for the art museum and some cheese steaks. "

"Right. I remember that quite well."

"Thalie took 'em to the Art Museum while I attended the board meeting on the Friday. My wife asked me why I didn't appreciate art, like you did, Thalie, you son of a bitch.

Thaleman chuckled. "School trips to the Art Museum in Denver – compared to you, I'm a connoisseur."

Walker continued, "Anyway, we went to the Philly production of A Chorus Line that Friday night – I couldn't believe a bunch of dancing homos could attract such crowds – the crowd was as excited as the Flyers crowd the night before. Takes all kinds I guess – that's gonna be a big issue in the armed forces someday. Anyway, my wife and Thalie and his wife really loved the show. We drove back to Washington on the Sunday afternoon. The three of them yacked the whole time about art and theatre – I couldn't get a word in edgewise."

"Yeah, you did, Big – remember when we got almost sideswiped by that big Cadillac?"

"God damn it, Thalie…"

Warrington raised his hands. "Okay, people. People! Let's just review a few more things here and then you generals can catch up with each other on old times. What do you recall about those Trust meetings, General Walker?"

"I don't recall much about the St Paddy day's meeting except that Sommerfeld wasn't able to attend so they dropped some agenda items. We only dealt with routine items. That pissed me off – I went all the way to attend the damn meeting for nothing. Well, the hot buffet was good."

"What about the October meeting?"

"The meeting in October was a big one."

"Why was that?"

"Sommerfeld announced he was leaving – wanted time to maybe make some changes in his life. Boy, you could almost hear the sighs of relief around the board table. He had always been such a difficult little bastard to deal with. And he had given the board some bad investment advice, on a tip. The Board found out MT had taken a significant investment loss. We had to decide to severely cut back on our student funding at the October meeting. So, it was good news, bad news. But the Trust never really recovered its losses that year and it's sort of in a suspended status ever since, hoping to receive some new donations."

Warrington took over again and said "Okay. Simon, do you recall anything from those two dates?"

With Warrington leading the questioning, Simon became sympathetic. "If you're looking for any relationship to the war gaming, I can say generally where we were at those two dates in 1980. By March 17, Lipson and I were finished pre-testing and had just decided our joint game would work three basic scenarios to try to get to a limited anti-ballistic defense stage without a serious loss of nuclear stability. In fact, now that I recall, some of us went out for green beer and dinner at Biff's in Arlington – I misplaced my briefcase at one point, but it turned up later at the bar - someone had turned it in from the booth they first showed us to, before we changed to a bigger one."

"Did you report that?"

"No – my briefcase was locked and anyway I didn't think there was anything important in it – just some code I was working on that no one else could have figured out. When I got home, I found a copy of a draft of an old and dated status memo on some aspects of the project but it was still stuffed in with some papers I had folded and had long since intended to shred. The fold didn't seem to have been disturbed in any way, so I figured no one had gone through it."

"Still, that was careless of you and technically a violation of the reporting rules for a missing briefcase."

Simon said, "Yeah, I guess. It was only missing an hour. I didn't want to bother anyone about it. In retrospect, I suppose I should have, but I might have been the one most bothered by it and I didn't have any time to lose for anything but the project. It was still behind schedule at that point."

"All the same, someone could have gotten into your briefcase and looked over those papers before it was returned to you.

"Theoretically, yes."

"Hmm. What about October 31st?"

"I can't recall anything, except someone had carved a pumpkin bearing a resemblance to Brezhnev. We were almost finished with the simulation runs with the Soviets at that point and about to write a final report. We already had a draft. I was upset that some DOD types were already starting to go full speed ahead with the idea of an ABM perimeter, despite the war gaming showing no net gain in security and considerable potential for nuclear destabilization."

"Because the Soviets could adopt some relatively easy and inexpensive counter measures against a partial ADM perimeter?"

"Well, it depended on how far we got – any real prospect of a future perimeter that could also overcome offensive countermeasures would very seriously destabilize. That was the gist of our back game findings in '80. Others would later advise it was probably not feasible anyway."

Sturgess gave the Generals and Kiss his biggest owlish look yet. "Did the President know you had actually back gamed with a Soviet group in 1980?"

Walker took that question. "No, we all agreed he didn't need to be informed and we thought we should not voluntarily come forward in case he might then have forbidden another back game - even if that could be very useful to military strategizing to avoid serious unnecessary destabilization. Indeed, that's the actual situation we may be facing now."

Sturgess pressed. "And the back gaming, without knowledge of the President. However convenient for the military, that approaches treason – you four, and anyone else knowing. That also makes you are all seriously vulnerable to blackmail."

"Well, that'd have to be the Soviets doing and we had as much on them, right up to Brezhnev. We made sure everyone on both sides playing the back-channel games knew their mutual risks."

"Except for our President."

"Well, in 1980, Carter sort of gave a go-ahead."

"'Sort of', and not passed on to the next sitting President. Alright, but who else, outside this room knows about the 1980 back game?"

Walker again answered, "Outside of two juniors reporting to me and Thalie, the only others in the loop were two reluctant exceptions: the guy I report to, now the Chairman of the Joint Chiefs of Staff, and the guy you two report to at the CIA, Richard Jansen. Then, when Simon took it to Toronto last year, we had to include more people - you guys I guess - at the CIA."

"Do you know that is everyone, for sure?"

"Yes – that was because no one else took our strategic war gaming seriously. Thought it was just an academic exercise. We didn't correct that misimpression."

"What about the key technical guys below you?"

'That would be Kiss and Lipson on the technical side and like I told you the one military report to me, one to Thalie. We haven't let them leave yet, in case we need to do it again."

"You let Dr. Kiss leave, though."

"Sure. It seemed a good way to further develop war gaming, off campus as it were. Too risky in the District here, right now." said Walker. He started another cigar.

"Okay, but it looks like Simon may have just been compromised up there, so where does that leave us?"

Walker turned his cigar a few times and said, "Well, it's progressed well up there otherwise. I think it means some more security measures, but otherwise, we want it to stay up there until we can get it safely back down here."

"Your concerns about the President's possible resistance to back games suggest that "back down here" could be after the end of the Reagan administration."

"Well, that might turn out to be the case." More turning of his cigar. "It could be that long. But if we get bad strategic destabilizing before that, even this President may want some better analysis of the dangerous counter-measure implications still affordable to the Soviets if we get anywhere close to a serious 'Star Wars' deployment."

Sturgess looked back at Simon.

"Is it possible in this ne gaming to obtain intelligence on the internal Soviet situation?"

Simon said, "Maybe, to the extent of whether there is unanimity versus dissensus on something strategically important – especially if the normal bell curve of consensus has become a bimodal disagreement, for example – but we must be very careful with that for two reasons."

"What are the reasons?" asked Warrington softly.

"Well, the first reason is that any real awareness of a disclosure of their internal psychological state – we explain it's just a pretesting methodology for useful games, not central to their interpretation - would scare them away from and prevent a back game to begin with. The second reason is that, in order to make use of that information on our side, they would have to be given similar information about us to make use of on their side."

Kiss waited for that to sink in with the CIA men.

"That is the nature of the back channel: my Soviet top technical and strategic counter-part, Ivan Tarasov, and I only agree to exchange the same kind of information between sides and the information must only be the minimum necessary to determine strategic nuclear destabilization potentials and measures to re-stabilize. It is not available otherwise for anybody else's offensive or defensive nuclear war plans."

"Okay," said Warrington.

"But couldn't even that be converted into an advantage?" said Sturgess.

Simon was irritated. "For Christ's sake you guys, do you think we are doing this for any other reason than to avoid some kind of horrendous nuclear exchange because one side stupidly thinks it may have some kind of temporary advantage?"

Warrington looked at Sturgess. They nodded their understanding, Sturgess reluctantly.

Sturgess said, "Alright gentlemen, I think we are satisfied with this interview. I imagine you will hear very soon from our superior, Mr. Jansen."

Walker said, "You will have to imagine it – I'm sure that son of a bitch will never tell you guys, even if he does follow up."

"Keeps us on our toes, sir," Warrington looked meaningfully at Kiss and Lipson, and, after waving Walker's cigar smoke away, he and Sturgess stood up and left the room.

Walker leaned over to the scientists and said, "Both of you will be tailed again from now on, likely by more than one agency, and security around you could become hard to take. Take it."

"Of course, General Walker," said Simon. "One final question to you: did you yourself try to test our security up there just prior to the Napoleon shutdown?"

"Nothing extra – no, damn it, we didn't. Maybe we should have."

"Now when and how do I get back to Toronto?" asked Simon.

"We have a flight arranged out of North Philadelphia Airport, directly back to, what's the local airport there this time, Thalie?"

"Kitchener Waterloo Regional this time."

"That's where the University of Waterloo is located?"

"Yes - we've built Simon a good reason for his sudden unexplained absence for Canadian police and intelligence or whomever - helping the University of Waterloo develop a new top secret something or other. They can say nothing of it."

Simon said "Okay, sounds plausible enough. I'm sure you will emphasize the "top secret" in the public news release."

"Smart ass," said Walker. "I gotta hand it you Simon – not just the smart guy, always the smart-ass guy."

"What about the flight timing?"

"Later today. Here's your Waterloo 'script'. Memorize the names, because certain people at the University of Waterloo will likely be called about it by certain other persons up there."

The Generals got up and left the room.

Lipson started to say something, but Simon put his finger to his lips.

When they were in the hallway, he said,

"Les, I'm sure that room is bugged. What did you want to say?"

"What do you think are the chances of a repeat?"

"If you mean a serious kiss, I have no idea yet, but Ivan is interested and I've got some good new results we can use this time, if there is one that can be run out of Toronto. The brass seems to agree with me that the District is the last place that can run a secure genuinely two-sided back channel nuclear war game at this point."

"Well, let's have lunch and you can give me some ideas for how to deal with Lover's problems here in the war games room at this point. At least, cold you turn off the red light – it is very irritating to the generals. God knows where this is headed but I will continue to follow your lead in whatever has to be done."

They headed out to one of the parking lots, getting to Lipson's car just as a heavy rain started.

"I say, we need a brolly," said Simon, in mock British.

"I'm surprised, you being in Toronto – shouldn't you always be carrying one," said Lipson, alluding to the city's British heritage?

"Oh, I think it's less British heritage now than American influence. Might leave us uncovered on a rainy day, though."

Chapter 14

After a period of being closed and then partly closed as a crime scene, Worlds was still experiencing sparse attendance on September 15th. Sabina Hurst had lunch there with Dee Proulx "to show the flag."

At lunch both agreed as Dee put it "to restore the momentum Worlds had up to the night of Keefe's death, and to ensure that would be recovered at least by the Halloween Ball. The event now assumed even greater importance for both.

They decided on a final program of events to fit Simon's gaming ideas through the rest of September and October up to and including Halloween that could restore confidence in the club including full restoration of the popular games in the arcade awaited Simon's hoped for return.

The next day Sabina met someone at a more anonymous place. She chose a busy Swiss Chalet on Yonge Street below Bloor.

She sat down at the back with an old friend of the family, Ray Russell. Russ was a burley guy with tussle of blond hair. He was a much sought-after private investigator by the Toronto well to do. He had gone to UCC with her father and had been retained from time to time by Hurst Associates.

Sabina didn't waste much time breaking bread with him.

"Russ, you busy?"

"Of course. You might check with your own law firm."

"Well, I hope you can make room for something even more important than that."

"Like what, Sabina?"

"I count on your total discretion."

"If we two can't have an off-the-record chat, I don't know who can."

"Good. Here's the problem. Simon Kiss is someone I care about. He's vital to the future of our family's amazing club and to my family's investment in it. I have reason to believe that Simon is being hounded by someone from his past who might want to destroy him or at least get to Rondo, his main computer program that includes profiling players' personalities to check reliability for games in the arcade."

"So,"?

"I want you to find out who that person is. It may or may not be connected to his previous work for the Pentagon – that remains an active issue for Simon and indeed that is probably behind his latest call-back by their military intelligence. This assignment could well deal with another side of his life. One that stresses him mentally."

"I don't know anything about the military intelligence side. That 'other side of his life' sounds like a tall order."

"Yes. And I have my own funds to pay you well for it."

"Funds or not, I have a loyalty to your family Sabina. Does your father know about this?"

"That is my one condition: no one else, including Dad, must know anything about this. The problem is that Simon could drop everything up here like a stone if he knew anyone was really onto his compromising personal stuff, if any of it is compromised."

"Including, drop you?"

"How perceptive of you, Russ."

She threw her napkin at him.

"Yes, I do have to admit a keen personal interest. And I care enough about him to be driven more by his own interest. It is in his interest that he be relieved of his past, once and for all. I don't think he can do it on his own. I think he needs some help. And I need yours."

They received their chicken salads and munched on them for a bit.

"Okay, I'm in. The cost is my usual $500 per day, plus expenses." Russ had his own family wealth, but he had found that $500 a day usually retained the most interesting work.

"Good."

"So where do I start?"

"Okay. Simon mentioned being funded through grad school at the University of Pennsylvania by a foundation called the 'Mathematics Trust.' It may now be mostly defunct, but I searched and I think it still has an office in Philadelphia. I need you to find out everything and anything about that organization in the last 10 years – since Simon was at grad school there in the early 1970's. There is something about the MT that he seems uneasy about. I think MT is where his enemy may be or at least was once. So, that's your first task."

"Find out about the Mathematics Trust and identify Simon's possible spook?"

"Yes, find out how that organization might be connected to Simon and then give that information to me for us to figure out our next step."

"Okay Sabina."

Russ slipped out as Sabina paid for lunch.

The next day, Russ landed at Philadelphia International Airport, admired the big photos of Grace Kelly, Joey Bishop and Silvester Stallone. He headed for a Sheraton hotel near the campus of the University of

Pennsylvania. It didn't take him long to discover the campus had a math and physics library.

Russ was there just after opening the next morning and poured over all sorts of stuff about the Mathematics Trust, cross-checking against names of grad students in math and physics at Penn in the early to mid-seventies. He picked up a connection to David Sommerfeld who was a grad student at Penn at the same time as Simon and had passed his PhD orals a year before Simon. There was no indication of Sommerfeld completing his doctorate. The man was a year later the Acting Executive Director of the Mathematics Trust, a position he held into the late seventies, before departing rather suddenly in 1978. Thereafter, the foundation had gone without an executive director and drastically reduced its annual student funding activity according to its latest annual report, dated 1980. Russ could not source an annual report after 1977.

Later in the afternoon, he walked over to the West Philadelphia offices of Mathematics Trust. It was a four-story converted residence along Walnut Street just west of 38th. A notice on the front door announced that admission to the premises was by appointment only. The place looked like it had been neglected for a while.

Russ walked around to the rear of the property. He noticed a clustered set of wires coming out of the ground and leading up to the second floor. He looked up and saw someone at the second-floor window.

He withdrew behind a protruding porch. He got out his camera and managed to take a close-up photo in reasonable light. He returned to the front of the building and crossed the street. He went down the block a bit, leaned against a lamppost and lit a cigarette. He didn't see any parked cars. Maybe whoever was there would come out eventually and could be followed and possibly even interviewed. He waited a few minutes.

At 5:15 a tall man slipped into the front door of the house. The same man slipped out at 5:24. Russ photographed and then tried to commit him to memory. He would remember enough of the man to identify him even without the photograph. He was certainly looking anxious, thought

Russ. He followed the man until the guy veered across Walnut Street through angry rush hour traffic. Russ figured he had enough photos and decided it might be better value to get back to his location outside the MT offices.

He had been right about that.

Ten minutes later, a stretch limo pulled up in front of the MT offices. Four well-dressed people got out and proceeded to the front door of the MT and let themselves in. Russ had taken photos and was prepared for a long wait.

He was rewarded sooner than he expected. Less than ten minutes later three police cars roared up the street and screeched to a halt, surrounding the waiting limo outside the MT offices. Police poured in the front door.

Russ waited around for a while. A few other police cars alarms screaming, screeched up, and an ambulance arrived. Then some press vehicles. He decided not to bother waiting any longer. He suspected he would read all about it in the newspapers the next day.

The next morning, taking breakfast in his room, he poured over the local newspapers. Philadelphia obviously cared a lot about its great university and any of its spin-off foundations, businesses and connected people. Certainly, any related events – toward or untoward.

What Russ had partly witnessed the day before was all over the front pages.

Four members of the Board of the Mathematics Trust had arrived at 5:25 p.m. to conduct a meeting that was to make the final Board decisions pursuant to a winding up of the foundation. When they entered the downstairs boardroom, they came upon the dead body of their legal counsel, one Barrington Stone.

Photos of a live Barrington Stone were featured on the front pages. The background coverage which followed in the main stories and side bars traced the recent circumstances of MT following some bad investment decisions in 1978 that had eventually resulted in the pending demise of the foundation. The bad investments had been championed by their last executive director, one David Sommerfeld, and had resulted in his departure from MT at the end of that year.

A photograph of Sommerfeld with other officials at an MT ceremony in 1978 presenting fellowship awards appeared in one of the papers. What equally caught Russell's attention was in the middle of one article that mentioned that the MT had sought in 1978 to reverse the American government's suppression for national security reasons of a scientific journal article by a former colleague of Sommerfeld and recipient of MT fellowship funding at the University of Pennsylvania. Simon Kiss' name as the former colleague was cited in that backgrounder – but there was no photo of Kiss.

Russ cursed himself for not obtaining a photo of Simon Kiss from Sabina Hurst. He had never actually seen or seen a photo of Simon Kiss in Simon's first year back in Toronto. Russ had simply forgotten to mention that to Sabina in his rush to get to Philadelphia.

One thing was clear to Russ, and he felt sure it would be borne out by his own photos: the man he had seen at the rear window of MT was a different man than the man he had seen enter and leave the place by the front door a short while later. And neither had looked like the photos of Barrington Stone.

Boy, thought Russ, Sabina has good hunches. The guy in his photo of the rear second story window sure looked like a slightly older David Sommerfeld in the one photo of the guy in a group photo he had seen at the Penn Math and Physics library.

But the man emerging at 5:24 was not the same man. He hadn't gotten around yet to look through class photos at the Penn Math and Physics library for others in Sommerfeld's grad years, including Simon Kiss. Russ decided he would stay in Philadelphia for a day or so to check for such photos and to see if anything new came out immediate police investigations and then fly back to Toronto.

Chapter 15

Earlier on the same day Russell had witnessed the events in Philadelphia, Simon had left his hotel in Annapolis at 12:00 p.m. in an unmarked Chevy. It was headed for Philadelphia's North Philadelphia airport where he would catch his pre-arranged CIA flight back to Ontario.

Halfway there the driver told him that the CIA plane would be 10 hours late. Without giving it much thought, Simon said, "Take me to West Philadelphia. I don't want to wait ten hours at the airport in North Philadelphia. On the whole, I would rather be in West Philadelphia," Simon said, taking liberties with W. C. Field's famous line about what his epitaph might say.

Simon concluded, "I'm sure I can find something interesting to do at the University of Pennsylvania, and you can enjoy Philly for a few hours yourself and pick me up later to drive us back to North Philadelphia."

"What'll I tell them? "

"That I am using the opportunity to catch up on a few journal articles not yet available in Toronto That, and that both of us will be having a long day."

The driver shrugged. He used his car phone to get the approval for Simon's change of plans. When it was finally given, they were already halfway to Philadelphia.

Simon was remembering the real reason this thought had come to him. He had been told at the conference in San Francisco that the Mathematics Trust which had funded him so amply at Penn was about to wind up with a final board meeting in Philadelphia on a date that he realized was this very day.

Simon had not been able since to make up his mind whether another big donation to the MT would be good money after bad. Maybe, he still thought, he could give them some last help – gift them a $million plus any proceeds from his suppressed article, should it become unsuppressed, and the rights become as commercially valuable, as Sommerfeld first thought. It might be enough for the creditors. After all, Simon did owe the MT foundation a lot for its early support of his graduate research.

He had started unsuccessfully to try to reach Big and the Board members with his idea and before he could pursue it further, he had been grabbed from Toronto. Maybe this was a chance to drop in on the MT just before or even at their final Board meeting. Anyway, he hadn`t been back to the Penn campus for several years.

When they got to the University of Pennsylvania stretch along Walnut Street in West Philadelphia, Simon told the driver to let him off at 34th street and pick him up there four hours later. That would still leave plenty of time to get to North Philadelphia airport.

Simon moved quickly along Walnut and across 38th Street and was standing at the front door of the Mathematics Trust at 5:15 p.m. On the way up from D.C. he had penned a short letter with his latest idea for helping save the Mathematics Trust in case he couldn't gain entry to the meeting. He had been right in surmising the door was now usually locked from the sign that was posted instructing that entry had to be arranged.

He tried the door and surprisingly it was open. He ignored the notice and went in.

There was a dusty smell inside. The late afternoon sun was beaming through a side window. It showed dusty air in its shafts. In the boardroom off the main entrance hall, a large table was neatly set for a meeting, indeed giving evidence the final board meeting of the Mathematics Trust would be proceeding on schedule.

From the voices he could hear upstairs Simon assumed some staff or Board members had already arrived. The voices got louder and angrier. Simon thought the better to interrupt anything that heated and laid his envelope on the board table.

He hesitated before leaving. He was sure he recognized one of the voices upstairs. It was David Sommerfeld. He heard the voice now shouting at, "It is the right of the Mathematics Trust to keep our copy of his article, goddamn it."

"That may be so, but not in your hands," were the angry words back at Sommerfeld from whomever he was arguing with.

"No. No, you don't know how to deal with this. Tell the Board that this is now in safekeeping and that will more than make up for my past mistakes. Just tell the Board that. It will help clear me of things the FBI chases me relentlessly about. They will understand even if you don't."

"No, again. Whatever that article's potential commercial value, there is no alternative but to liquidate the Trust assets now. I will not let you leave here without speaking to the Board directly about it. They'll be here in a few minutes."

"I'm not going to talk to them with you counseling them against me, you bastard. But if you want me to stay, I will tell them you were the one who brought to me those stupid investment tips, you and your secret source at Wharton and your goddamned Main Line friends."

"How dare you – I paid you handsomely to shut up. What will they say when they find that out?"

"They will say, 'Who paid you to pay me to shut me up and why?' you idiot. God, you're stupid. No thanks for suggesting it."

"Sommerfeld, you've carried on with these insults and threats long enough. I want you to spare the Board your further insults. Get out of here or I'll throw you out."

The sounds upstairs indicated a physical struggle had begun and the altercation was approaching the top of the main stairs. Simon hastily grabbed the envelope back from the board table and made a quick exit out the front door.

He moved rapidly along Walnut Street and crossed dangerously through honking rush hour traffic over to the campus of the University of Pennsylvania where he found a bench outside the math and physics building.

A half hour before, David Sommerfeld had looked out one of the rear windows at MT. He was in the midst of desperately trying to find a copy of Simon Kiss' suppressed article for the Journal, 'Decision and Theory', that was part of the theoretical basis for the Rondo program for computerized war gaming. He had been a fool not to emphasize more to the Board when he was the Executive Director of MT that there was large potential public good and commercial value from the article, and that might be realized under the participation agreements made with students funded by the foundation. He was sure the long-term value of the article could be worth a lot to MT. Then he had been a fool to accept the investment tip from the foundation's legal counsel, Barrington Stone, to make up for the recent diminishing value of the foundation's investments. After all, it came from the "best inside sources."

It made him furious he had simply been asked to leave because he had "failed in his performance." The Board had itself failed to pick up on positive value and had not asked for due diligence on the investment proposals except from that given by their smiling legal counsel, Barrington Stone, the man behind the bad investment tips in the first place.

Neither of those were Sommerfeld's fault. But then, Sommerfeld had never been able to extricate himself from things that seemed to be "his fault." When he was in grade three, another kid had stripped, run around naked and Sommerfeld got blamed for it. When he was in grade ten, a car had been pushed onto a railway track and had almost caused a huge tragedy. There were a whole bunch of guys that did it, but he was singled out because the only kid giving any evidence had said he could only remember Sommerfeld calling out "push'" When he was at Penn in his graduate year, he was given a statistics exam not based on the course he had received. It was a subject he had always argued with his professors about. He failed it and he was then told to abandon his doctorate. There was even a position arranged for him, if he wished, with the Mathematics Trust.

The thing that had eaten away at him all the time at Penn was the 'swishers,' the guys that just seemed to swish through all the tests and, to their professors' excitement had luckily sunk the doctoral basketball cleanly through the net for a three-pointer from outside the damn paint.

Sommerfeld knew he was as smart as any of the best, but that he was not a swisher. His mind was always cluttered with too many ways of thinking about problems. And just before he left Penn, he finally had admitted to himself that one or two of the best students weren't just swishers. Simon Kiss was the one he was always the most jealous of. Kiss had always irritated him the most.

He had seen Kiss at lunch one day and went over to apologize for carrying on about "certain swisher colleagues" only to find Simon deep in melancholia after the death of his girlfriend, Donna Meyer.

Simon had looked at him in a way Sommerfeld could never forget – a completely blank stare. It was as if he wasn't even there. Simon had only said "let's keep in touch," took Sommerfeld's new phone number at MT that he hastily scrawled on a napkin and left the table. Sommerfeld vividly recalled how Simon had headed slowly, almost aimlessly out of the lunchroom as if he were still in shock – he actually collided with some people coming into the room. It was only a few weeks later that Sommerfeld learned Simon had probabl6 suffered a nervous breakdown that week. With the input of a graduate behavioral psychology course Sommerfeld was taking, he wondered if he could use this deep knowledge of Simon in several later contacts with him. The fact was he had taken advantage of the deeply disturbed guy and kind of hypnotized him to stay in contact.

Now, Sommerfeld had let himself into the MT on the foundation's last legal day by a basement window which he had used a few times before when he worked there and had forgotten a key. He heard the front door being unlocked and someone entering.

Sommerfeld had hoped to have been through printing the Kiss article and out of MT before anyone knew the better.

And then, there was that bastard, Barrington Stone, staring at him.

Les Lipson wondered what the hell was up. He had been called to the Pentagon war games room. It no longer was disturbed by a flashing red light, but the expression on General Walker's face was a close substitute.

"Sit down Les. Do you know anything about this?" Walker tossed some Philadelphia newspapers at Lipson.

"What, a murder in Philadelphia?"

Uh oh, Lipson thought - it was at the Mathematics Trust.

"Why would I?"

"Because it damn well happened when we at least know that Simon Kiss was there yesterday, and it involves stuff and people he knows about, including me, and you maybe know about it, that's why!"

"I have no knowledge of Simon being in Philadelphia, yesterday." Lipson said as he checked the date on the newspapers, "As far as I know, he left Annapolis when we did, headed for North Philadelphia airport."

"Well, the CIA plane out of there was delayed ten hours so he went on to spend the rest of the afternoon and early evening in West Philly. I never would have allowed it, but he got an approval from lower down. Everything around Kiss seems to be going to shit these days. That can't happen in our operations. I want your estimate on what we have to do and what extra costs we face if we bring him back in for good and do the next back-channel games entirely here."

"Bring him in, for good?"

"Well, for a good long time."

"I can give you some implications now, but I would have to do some work before I could give you anything like a report."

"Fine, tell me what you can, now. Get me a report to me by the end of tomorrow."

"Well, on the downside, the first thing that we could lose is Simon Kiss."

"There's no way he could escape our grasp."

"I don't mean that – I mean a Simon Kiss who is still highly motivated to do his work with us."

"What do you mean?"

"Oh, come on, sir. Have you ever heard of working to rule?"

"You mean he would withdraw his best services – I would give him orders in that case. Who does he think he is?"

"Who do you think you are?"

"Never mind!"

"Well, I do mind, because you asked me for my sense of what would happen under exactly that attitude and that scenario, and I am giving you my best advice. It would not go well with Simon and I'm not sure what we would get from him. But it would likely be far less than when he is fully motivated, as he seems to be in Toronto."

"What about getting him all the same capabilities, here?"

"Well for starters we have agreed for some time that is the main reason he is in Toronto – his set-up with the university and the club there have given him a large set of players and plays that we probably couldn't achieve safely here early on or at all. This is too hot a place. It takes too long to assemble the control groups, never mind the active players. The cost and alone of duplicating all of that would be beyond our capability - anyone's capability – and be tricky at best from a security standpoint. Frankly, it's too late if you want something in the next few months brought back here and replacing what we have in Toronto with Simon fully motivated."

"Okay, then we're back to where we were when he left - we will have to secure what we have up there better and, at the same time, figure out how to move it back here as soon as possible."

"Yeah, that sounds like a better plan, except, I wonder how we can get away with another genuine backchannel game like we did in 1980 with the Soviets, anywhere? It's a much different Kremlin and a much tighter and centralized place in Washington under Reagan than it was during the Carter presidency. We can only do it if Simon and Tarasov conclude we can."

"Okay, a lot of our successful back-channel operations during previous wars were outside America. They had to be, to make meaningful contact with the enemy. We're still in a Cold War."

"Maybe the tensest moment."

"But you know, having it up in Toronto takes a lot of the fun out of it for me," said Walker.

"And I'm sure you realize that Toronto makes it far more interesting to the CIA. What you may have to bring off is persuading someone higher up to make sure it is understood by whomever necessary, but not beyond that person, that it has top military strategic value and should have an ample budget even outside our boundaries."

"I'm thinking Les, you and Simon had more of a chance to talk at Annapolis than we or the CIA have a record of."

"If we did, the whole project of basing strategic decisions on a good sense of the other side is the better for it."

"Okay. I continue to hope you're right. I'll do my part. Just make sure things around here function again without some sense of imminent crisis. The President wants a new round of our own strategic gaming within the month, and I want genuine back gaming to support us before the red phone rings on his desk."

"Okay, that puts time pressure on what we've got up in Toronto. I'll arrange for Simon to get going on it, now that I've had a good talk with him and then report to you."

"And Les, I want Kiss to be able to sign off on what's up with that Anatol Rapoport up there. He's on the CIA list of anti-American intelligence risks and there are reports he has been copied on Simon's runs at the University of Toronto computer center."

"Oh hell. Okay. I'll figure something out with Warrington and Simon.".

Chapter 16

Simon arrived at Buttonville Airport north of Toronto via Waterloo Region airport after a flight from North Philly. He was the sole passenger on a two-engine Beach Craft. It helped to substantiate his cover story with Toronto police that he had been suddenly needed to work on a top-secret government project at the University of Waterloo.

Simon decided not to bother yet catching up on his sleep and took a limo into the city to the back lane entrance to Worlds. It was just after 5:00 a.m. He got out of the car and entered the club with his back door key as rapidly and unnoticed as he had exited it four days previous.

He went to his office, and despite wanting to stay awake, nodded off at his desk.

Predictably, the first to see him so suddenly again in his office was Powell, at 7:15 that morning.

"I keep welcoming you back these days, Dr. Kiss."

"Yes. I'm glad to be back, again to pick up the arcade situation and finish the plans for the Halloween ball." He rubbed his eyes. "Did you see the police with the energy bar package and your further recollections?"

"Yes. They seemed to appreciate their importance."

"Ah, then, that is very helpful Powell."

"Alas, sir, I am now guilty of a serious error with them. They have twisted my statements that you and Sabina worked closely on some of the club's affairs to question whether the two of you were linked romantically. You know how the police can be. I regret ever having mentioned you and Sabina in the same sentence?"

"Well, I'll put in a word with the Hursts to go no further than a tar and feathering – you can wear that to the Halloween Ball."

"I can't imagine how you can save me. As Porter, I am expected to be the height of discretion. That serious an indiscretion is grounds for firing me."

"Anyway, Mr. Hurst is aware of your irreplaceable intelligence role here."

"Thank you, sir."

Powell departed.

Simon concentrated first on what additional details of his cover story he would have to concoct when pressed by Sabina and her father about his "having been rushed to the University of Waterloo for some secret work." They likely guessed eventually it had been the Pentagon leash, but his and their pretense had to be otherwise. A knowing if distasteful look to go along would be sufficient.

He left a voice message for Sarto to drop by and looked at the phone messages on his desk. Most of them were to call Miservy at the Metropolitan Toronto Police Department. He knew he would have to face another interview. He decided better sooner than later and called police headquarters.

As he did so, an e-mail came from Ivan. In an apparent reference, it read:

"First tests passed, here and hopefully there,"

This was good news to Simon - some form and degree of backchannel nuclear back game was a go on the Soviet side and that

Tarasov's contacts there were accepting that security of core secrets in Toronto had been tested without a loss of cover, despite Keefe's death at Worlds.

Russell was also back in Toronto at noon that day. He spotted Sabina already seated at the back of the Swiss Chalet and headed for her. He had his report and the photos he had taken.

Sabina nodded as he sat down.

"So, Russ. I suppose you've heard that the MFD technology Executive Director Martin Davies was murdered in the tunnels at Queen's Park"

"Yeah, terrible. I read about that on my plane in. It begins to look like something big and bad is happening,"

"I wonder. Go get some chicken and then you can tell me what you have got."

"The chicken can wait." He summarized his report, saying "It's quite a story in Philly, with no conclusion in sight. The police there have a suspect and a warrant out for his arrest. A guy named Sommerfeld – apparently connected somehow with Simon from university days.

Russ handed Sabina his photos, explaining "the first guy at the back window is Sommerfeld, not the same guy as leaving by the front."

Sabina tried to remain calm as she looked at the photos.

"Russ, have you ever actually seen Simon Kiss, or a photo of him."

"No, I should have mentioned that. He's only been in Toronto for a few months. It was something I was going to check. I didn't think I would have any urgent reason for it until I got back here. Geez - why do you ask, Sabina?" He inwardly kicked himself.

"The photos you took of the man leaving the Mathematics Trust…" She paused.

"Yes?" he asked.

"Russ, that was Simon!"

Chapter 17

Simon was mentally processing the murder of Martin Davies. They had renewed their acquaintance in Toronto but not their once close student friendship. Both shared a belief in the potential public policy applications of computer assisted psychologically pretested strategy gaming. It had facilitated the negotiations with MFD. Even during the negotiations with MFD, that was the only one on one personal conversation Simon had with Davies. But he thought about it now, still shaking his head as he stuffed the newspaper in a waste basket and headed to the office of the Chief of Detectives, Colin Miservy.

He could see Miservy in his inner office surrounded by several other detectives. He caught his eye. Miservy waved away all but one of the others in his office and beckoned Simon to come in.

"Good morning, Dr. Kiss. Please sit down. Coffee?" Simon fixed a cup from the set-up on the table.

"I needed another interview after the Davies death."

"Yes." Simon said quietly.

"I know we asked you here to complete our interviews with you about Keefe's death, but let's kill two birds with one stone. Sorry, that isn't appropriate."

"No."

Simon sipped his steaming coffee.

"Okay then, some of our questions to you about Keefe also apply to a to Davies' death. Martin Davies was known to you, wasn't he? It seems now that he was the intended victim in Keefe's death. It turns out he, knowingly or unknowingly, gave Keefe the poisoned energy bar. We suppose whoever the murderer is has likely now gotten to his intended victim. So, the deaths are likely related. Anyway, we have not tied off your relationship with the MFD Ministry. Did you for example do any direct work for MFD?"

"No. Mr. Hurst was about to do some executive consulting. But that didn't happen, after Keefe's death. And, of course, they partially fund what I am doing at Worlds"

"Was the grant up for renewal or anything?"

"No, it ran for the next two years."

What contacts have you ever had with Martin Davies?"

"Well, we attended The University of Pennsylvania at the same time. He helped negotiate the technical side of the funding agreement, along with two lawyers. Only one or two friendly conversations since then when he would come to the club along with the Minister and others from MFD on Tuesday nights."

"What were the friendly conversations about?"

"The one I remember was how strategy gaming models might be used in policy applications."

"What policy applications?"

"Oh, anything, I guess, from ending poverty to the price of electricity."

"Those are big issues."

"Yes, but our conversations were only theoretical - never anything immediately useful."

"What else?"

"What do you mean, 'what else'?"

"Can you think about anything else about Martin Davies?"

"Nothing since student days at Penn where I knew him a bit."

Simon figured they would find out about that anyway.

"What was your relationship there?"

"Well, he was a bright guy. Based on our few contacts, I liked him. I suppose you could say in our shared progressive public policy interests we were kindred spirits. But we were acquainted, not really close friends."

"Okay, let's finish off about Minister Keefe. We want to ask you again why he would take such an interest in the crash of your gaming that night."

"Well, we can assume his note "*Napoleon disparu*" related to that. Maybe he was already concerned about somebody trying to get at our co-property?"

"That seems to be the root motive in all this. Again, do you have any ideas – any, at all - on who that might be?"

"Only generally. I mean that it is likely seen as a valuable property from many viewpoints including commercial. I'm sure there is an interest in the foreign policy community. We've had several above-board approaches for partnerships. Some people are trying to model the election process with behavioral psychology a la Madison Avenue to voters. Heaven knows what interest there may be below board. Roy Hurst and our two silent private partners agree with my view that we are not yet at a point where we want to release anything to anyone else or get to an open platform stage for the Rondo gaming software. That's still in the future.

"Who are the silent partners?"

"I'd prefer not to mention. We didn't really need additional financing, but multiple participation always helps to legitimize closely held ventures. Anyway, they would have the least interest in revealing or exposing the Rondo property in a way that would diminish its current investment value."

"Sorry, Dr. Kiss, but this is part of a murder investigation."

Simon shrugged and mentioned two names.

"So, I assume you've been investigating the identity of Mr. X that night."

"Dead end so far. There were five at the oil table that night. The new guy who had arranged earlier in the day to join them that night was one Wilson Seymour, with Texaco. He was supposed to be their new Personnel Director up here. Big guy, maybe six four. He said he loved to play games. But the others couldn't recall his specific movements away from their table because they were intently concentrating on the war game they were playing."

"This alleged new Personnel Director was never at Texaco, here or in the States. Only told the others he had come up from the States the day before. They just accepted him as their guest on trust. When people asked about his background, he was vague. Something about a master's degree in chemical engineering from Ohio State University and most of career with Texaco. We contacted Ohio State and there's no record of anyone with that name ever attending or receiving a degree."

Simon said, "So, you're at a loss as to who Mr. X was."

"No other leads. Only thing people recall is he was a big guy."

Chapter 18

Kent Maddow loomed large at his desk, as he stretched his arms out to steady his conflicting thoughts. He was considering what to do next in Toronto.

Martin Davies had finally been taken out of the picture, but that left an even more exhaustive investigation in Toronto that could get to Sommerfeld and exposure back to himself. That had been compounded now that the Philadelphia police had an arrest warrant out for Sommerfeld in connection to the homicide at the Mathematics Trust. Even without that, Sommerfeld was a serious problem because he too would realize he had been duped, and there was likely at least one phone call from Sommerfeld that could ultimately be traced to Maddow in Houston.

Maddow could probably avoid any direct criminal tie-in. But he still wanted an opportunity somehow to get at Kiss' vulnerability. Now he had heard the rumor from his inside sources in the Pentagon that new nuclear war gaming was commencing. Knowing that, he concluded it was likely that another back game with the Soviets would be attempted, this time out of Toronto. He knew Tarasov had been Simon's Soviet partner in the 1980 nuclear game. Sommerfeld had previously gathered enough from Davies that indicated the full capability was buried in Simon Kiss' software at Worlds. He had also recently confirmed that Tarasov was still in Canada.

An idea and then a plan began to germinate. If a new back game was begun out of Toronto, could the secrecy of the back channel be seriously compromised. He now knew enough about its basics via Davies and Sommerfeld that he could build his own version of the psychologically pre-tested gaming methodology. It would take him a year, with enough resources to which he had access to, and paid players to test it. That could be expedited – if Sommerfeld stayed loyal to the group. That was now Maddow's immediate problem. Could he trust Sommerfeld?

If he could count on Sommerfeld, he came up with a scheme that would fatally expose the back channel and Simon Kiss himself for at least several months or at least long enough for Maddow to duplicate Kiss' current strategy gaming platform. Maddow's right-wing partners would pay richly for adapting it into voter and election modeling, and he himself would likely rake in as much or more using it to model oil industry public relations scenarios. All the while he would be positioning himself also to break into the lucrative international strategy business with conflict resolution software.

The next day in Toronto, Sommerfeld received a hand delivered secret instruction from Maddow. He was surprised when he saw the lengths the group was prepared to go to expose Kiss. It would indeed likely sideline Kiss for a while at least and give the group time to replicate enough of the Rondo platform for other peaceful uses. He could see the plausibility of the group thinking that Sommerfeld could significantly help them do that. And they knew he was also now implicated in the Philadelphia murder investigation. Accepting Maddow's scheme and continuing undercover in Toronto would buy him time to figure out how to get himself out of Maddow's now surely bloody claws.

Two days after that, Sommerfeld, playing his dutiful role, called on the latest phone number. He left a message: "Terrific property strategy. I concur with all points. Have secured control of the necessary real estate for the required period. Next project proceeding as planned. Await funding by usual channel."

When he received Sommerfeld's confirming phone message indirectly via his deliberately attenuated network, Mallow sat back in his leather chair and smiled.

So much for Simon Kiss and the backchannel, he thought.

Part Four:
October 1983

Chapter 19

Blend a bellflower blue sky with a billion blazing leaves rustling in a west wind, millions loosed to dance their way to the ground through the still mild air, and you have an autumn day in Ontario that dazzles the senses.

October 5, 1983, was thusly blessed when the 32nd Session of the Legislative Assembly of Ontario resumed sitting after its summer adjournment. The resumption of the sitting suddenly and surprisingly involved only one voting item. It was put to the vote of the Legislature, after which the Session was summarily prorogued the same day by the approved motion of Premier Margaret Stephenson.

She rose on the first item of business, "Announcements," to formally advise the Legislature of the deaths in recent days of the Minister of Finance and Development, the Honorable Michael Keefe, the Executive Director of Technology in the Ministry of Finance and Development, Martin Davies. She gave suitable summaries of the life and importance of these essential public figures. The Opposition leaders then added their respectful comments. The Premier again arose, thanked them, and continued,

"Mr. Speaker, may I further inform this House that, yesterday, I was officially informed by the head of the joint team of the Ontario Provincial Police and Metropolitan Toronto Police that these untimely deaths are being investigated as linked homicides."

Although this possibility had been all over the news, her official confirmation of the deaths related to homicides prompted much noise in the Legislature. The Speaker took a few minutes to bring things under control.

The Premier announced that, due to the disruption the police investigations would cause, she was moving the proroguing of the current Legislative Session with the plan of opening a new session on the last Tuesday of October. Before she could finish her words, there were howls of protest from the Opposition benches.

Finally, she was able to resume, with her justifications.

"Mr. Speaker, thank you for returning this house to some semblance of order. I wish to set out several points regarding my motion to prorogue. First, my decision is subject to the approval of the Lieutenant Governor, which I will be seeking forthwith. Second, I ask that the leaders of the Opposition Parties meet with me immediately following today's adjournment in the Premier's Office for a more detailed review of the Government's unprecedented situation. The fact is the police investigations underway mean some of our central agency offices and too many of our current files are currently frozen and not accessible for normal use. In that regard, I wish to advise the Legislature that I have today asked Ottawa, and they have agreed that the Royal Canadian Mounted Police assume primary charge for the investigation of any criminal charges surrounding the deaths of Minister Keefe and Martin Davies."

She allowed for a further noisy moment in the house.

"Please. There is more. My Government has concluded that for the Ministries and central agencies of the Ontario Government to fully cooperate with the intense investigation that now must be undertaken, I do not want the major time and resources that will have to be devoted to that investigation to compromise or be compromised by the normal public procedures during a Legislative sitting or even resumption of Legislative Committee work. Hence, I have made my motion to prorogue. My action is with my express undertaking that our starting point for the new Session will still be today's Throne Speech in th4 hands of the

Lieutenant Governor, not with any new proposals, again an unusual commitment. I can help gain the Opposition's full cooperation on a quick way forward under the circumstances, which I will share with them and the House leaders when we meet in the next few minutes.

The Opposition asked for a half-hour recess, which the House unanimously agreed to and the Speaker granted.

Forty-five minutes later, each Opposition leader arose to criticize the prorogation in principle. But each chose to sympathize with Government given the unprecedented circumstances and referred to the Premier's various reasons and promises. They yielded without further debate to a vote to prorogue the Parliamentary Session, which the Governing Party did not have to use its majority to win. The shortest sitting of the Provincial Legislative session in Ontario history was ended, and the current Parliamentary Session was officially prorogued the next day, with the Lieutenant Governor's consent.

Over the next several days, numerous police force members began to filter through Queen's Park – some in uniform guarding sensitive offices, others in suits doing the actual investigating and interviewing. Because of the large scope of MFD responsibilities for which Keefe was responsible, there were various possible lines of inquiry across the Government stretching even beyond the Government's central agencies and largest Ministry. The Premier had been right – the extensive investigations were an unprecedented significant disruption to the normal course of Government.

By the last week in October, Colin Miservy was deputed to sum up progress at a high-level combined force meeting in the sound-proofed MFD boardroom. His voice was strained. He looked tired.

"Frankly, our investigations in the Ontario Government have turned up very little we did not know. We thank the Ontario government for fully cooperating in this investigation. It did indeed significantly impede their normal operations."

Miservy repeated that at a press conference an hour later.

He faced questions.

The first one cut to the chase "We know about Mike Keefe, but what do you know about Davies? Who was he? How did he get into the Ontario Public Service? Wasn't he already a controversial figure?"

Miservy replied, "Martin Davies was the late Executive Director of Technology Development at the MFD. We had been trying to reach that gentleman a few days before he died for an interview about Minister Keefe's death. He was highly qualified for his position, but he had a somewhat controversial background before entering the Ontario public service. He was falsely accused of Communist connections and fired from Cal Tech in the early 1970s. His career resumed here in Toronto, where he avoided the military draft in the late Viet Nam years when the Los Angeles Times published articles exposing those false accusations. He was then hired as a professor at Ryerson and, after that, competed successfully for his position at MFD. He said he was proud to live in Ontario and thought MFD was an innovative Ontario Ministry."

The question was even harder: "Why is your investigation of two such high-profile homicides stalled"?

All Miservy could answer was, "Sorry, the current conduct of the investigation is confidential." It left the impression the investigation was indeed stalled.

Then he had to field the toughest question."

"It has been learned that Davies' was in contact with someone named David Sommerfeld – a man on an "active" file of the FBI - a guy once associated with Simon Kiss at Worlds. What can you tell us about Sommerfeld – he's involved in a recent homicide investigation in Philadelphia, isn't he?"

"Yes, he I a person of interest. We have been trying to locate Sommerfeld. The FBI is on that."

The last question Miservy ducked because it was one those shouted at him after ending the press conference: "Doesn't all involve Simon Kiss?"

Chapter 20

Simon Kiss pulled his car into the long driveway to his large farmhouse at Lakeview. He was accompanied by a chatty passenger, Anatol Rapoport.

Rapoport was a captivating polymath professor at the University of Toronto. He was a Russian-born American who had studied long and hard to become a concert pianist in Vienna in the 1930s before Nazism chased him back to America. He obtained a mathematics degree from the University of Chicago in 1941 and, after serving in the war, became a leading figure in behavioral science, including the application of game theory to human behavior and its empirical testing in laboratory experiments.

Rapoport had been a strong opponent of the American war in Viet Nam. He left the U.S. to become a professor of psychology and mathematics at the University of Toronto in 1970. Currently, Rapoport was the Director of the Institute for Advanced Studies in Vienna, but he frequently returned to the U. of T. as his base university.

Simon had explained to Rapoport that they were being "allowed" to spend a weekend together at Lakeview by American intelligence. This was because Simon had said he would use the weekend to get to the bottom of Rapoport's possibly illicit interest in Simon's work and then report it and, if necessary, help prevent any further "tricks" by Rapaport.

As they left the car, Rapoport asked bluntly, "Are we free to talk here – is your place bugged?"

"I sweep it every day according to instructions given to me by my security guy."

Cliff, the houseman, drove the car with their bags over to the garages. Cliff's wife, Mable, opened the door with a welcoming smile and admitted them.

Simon showed Rapoport around the main floor. When they arrived at the conservatory, Rapoport spotted the piano at one side of the tremendous glassed-in room and said,

"I see a delightful Toronto Heintzman Grand – indeed, it is one of their rare full grand pianos. Will you allow me to play? I think the Rondo Allegro in Beethoven's Piano Sonata #8, in C minor."

"The Pathetique - it would be a perfect introduction to the pathetic purpose of our weekend to expose human frailty."

For the next few minutes, all of Lakeview was pervaded by Rapoport's brilliant piano playing.

As he lowered his hands from the last notes, Rapoport said, "Nothing like four repetitions at the end of a small symphony, eh Simon?"

"Five would be too much—six, as in some other, insufferable compositions.

Then they returned to the matters at hand. During the drive to Lakeview, Rapoport had explained his monitoring of some of Simon's early results at the U of T computer room had been mainly a "signal of my strong and admiring interest." He explained he could only pick up something he could use without discussing it at some length with Kiss.

Simon had asked him, "Why didn't you just come and tell me in person?"

Rapoport had chuckled. "At that point, more American spooks were following me than are likely following you – I was still working full-time in Vienna. Anyway, you have my word that I am interested."

Rapoport filled Simon in on his recent background and the latest developments in the European social science world. He had not found much "hard" quantitative social science or a genuine peace and war analysis and conflict resolution initiative in Europe. Rapaport explained that he had returned to the U of T, where he thought there was a better chance.

Now he said, "I always ask a question of uncomprehending people: Is peace simply the temporary absence of the lustful competitive behavior of war, or can peace become a more actively cooperative and equally lusty human motivation?

"Little did I know there was already someone here, much my junior, you, who had already done more interesting behavioral science work on actual peace and war gaming based on cooperation emergence than I had ever been able to do in my lab projects. Alas, my experiments validating the 'tit for tat' solution were mostly with university kids. Yours have been with cooperative generals and at the Worlds Club are with accomplished strategic government and business thinkers. I am eager to see where you are in the empirical science of strategy games, Simon."

After dinner, in the conservatory, Simon himself played the Mozart Rondo back to Rapoport well enough for Rapoport to ask,

"And you say you are not much trained?"

"I only trained through high school. But, well, I just heard you play it."

Rapoport laughed hugely.

"And indeed, you call your software, 'Rondo,' among other things, a musical term."

"Yes. The name fits what it does – it combines the mathematical theory of games with a continuing empirical experiment in how people on teams actually play games. My hypothesis being tested is that barring external situational shocks, cooperation emerges, and cooperative strategy games stabilize or do not after six definable moves in a given dynamic game stage, based on the intersection of various key behavioral vectors in the game's strategic space. I haven't written anything publicly since some of that was to be published in a post-doctoral article still suppressed by the U.S. military. But it is consistent with your own recent "tit for tat" solution to the emergence of cooperation between players in strategy games. It's more like a Rondo Reverso structure – the repeating theme is discovered in later moves, not in the introductory move. But I just left it at Rondo, which is a bit misleading."

"Well, that's brilliant work, Simon. I assume it is replicable. If so, it adds much dynamic behavioral context to my simple "tit for tat" logical solution and any of Nash's mathematical solutions to conflicting sides. I recall reading somewhere that you may discover the first constant in quantitative social science?"

"That's hype – somebody said that who should not have revealed anything about it a few years back in my 1972 journal article and called me in from the Rand Corporation. They had a copy of the article, and it was almost leaked before the DOD's order was approved. But remember, the Rondo form is only a special case. It does not stabilize like that empirically if there are shocks in the external situation, which is often the case. In that case, my point is that such normal shocks, in theory, begin another six-stage dynamic game – my experimental games can avoid an external shock, such as big economic changes or random exogenous events. When I inject those into my games, I observe them for any additional pattern other than they defaulted back to square one. I can't find any learned behavior that spills over from stage to stage. It's as if a whole new group takes over for each side, neither with any background from previous stage games by their sides." And that's with the same group of bright kids.

"But even the six-move maximum behavioral interval in the absence of shock, if others can validate it, is a breakthrough. It suggests a whole new game has begun somehow if cooperation or resolution has not transferred between the previous game stages."

"Yeah, you've got it, Anatol, and I'm still struggling with that 'interval. In the meantime, we are about to have another guest this afternoon. He may be a little dusty – one of our gardeners."

Ivan Tarasov had appeared at the door to the conservatory, indeed in a dusty state.

"Most of the fall bulbs have been planted, sir."

Then he turned and said, "Hello, Anatol."

"Well, if it isn't Ivan Tarasov. I met you last at the Institute of Applied Social Science in Salzburg."

"My deligh6ful background with both of you is why I'm in disguise. There's more than one plain sedan with dark-suited men and binoculars."

The men shook hands, and Simon bid them talk in the less visually exposed kitchen.

Simon was smiling broadly. "I didn't realize you two knew one another. But then, as I think of it, I shouldn't be too surprised. Ivan and I go back a while – we first met at a conference in '75. Ivan seemed to know some of what I was doing at the time. At first, I thought he was simply a clever Soviet intelligence gatherer. But then I learned he was involved in tricky backchannel traffic between the Soviets and the West. I soon discovered that we were social scientists with similar academic backgrounds and interests."

"In fact," said Tarasov, "I modeled the last years of my university and post-grad development around Simon - the KGB tracks who are the best American graduate students in fields of interest and what they're up to."

Simon said, "You know, you never told me that, Ivan. So now we know that all three of us are, shall we say, kindred spirits."

"With an emphasis on the spirits, surely, eh, Anatol," Ivan laughed as he accepted a second glass of vodka from Simon and toasted them both.

Simon asked, "Ivan, did you know Anatol would be here? Please tell me you did not."

"I arrived here this morning with the landscapers as you and I planned. I could now see and hear him playing the piano in the conservatory. Do our friends in the dark sedan know he is here?"

Rapoport answered, "Yes – well, too of them anyway. They have been told I am spending the weekend here to enable Simon to find out 'what I know' and what commie mischief I'm up to."

"Aha, and Simon exaggerated what should have taken him a few minutes to provide into a need for you to spend a whole weekend together."

"Exactly," said Anatol.

The men laughed.

"You are both, like me, blessedly incorrigible," said Simon, raising a glass to them. Let's go downstairs to my office for some serious talk before Ivan must leave with the last landscaping truck."

As they entered Simon's office, it was Tarasov's turn to admire the computer set-up. He whistled softly as Simon explained again to him as he had to Rapoport, its connectivity to both mainframes at the U of T and Worlds Club.

Chapter 21

The three men sat down in the sectional sofa arrangement, and Simon poured more drinks from the bottles he had brought downstairs.

Simon explained his honest attempt with Ivan to back game the nuclear situation between American and Soviet Generals, this time on an even riskier basis, with only one Soviet General in on it.

"I asked Anatol, of course in strictest confidence, to help us evaluate the final version of the psychological part of our latest software, and he accepted. That's why I wanted him here this weekend."

Rapoport said, "My question to you, Ivan is the same as I put to Simon: if your one or more protectors know you have additional knowledge not only on the destabilizing conditions but the moves that might lead to their side's gains or losses in strategic nuclear position, can you trust them not to try to drag that extra information out of you? What you are about to do is very dangerous for both of you."

Tarasov said, glancing at Simon, "Well, we arranged that the backchannel data not pertinent to stabilization conditions could not be accessed by one side without automatically giving it to the other side. That worked last time. Not only that, a condition of backchannel gaming is that either of us can instantly and permanently destroy the whole thing, so the back gaming cannot be usurped by our users, including our protectors. In essence, we feed each side only the sequence of moves and countermoves that most indicate they maintain stability. That then becomes an option in the rest of their gaming."

"Yes," confirmed Simon. "Even the data shareable between Ivan and I will require an elaborate exchange of passwords we have devised. Mind you, the whole thing depends entirely on our complete trust. This time the core program of th3 software we use is at Worlds in Toronto, which is transferable here if breached there, and vice versa.

"Anyway, if the core is destroyed, it would take even me, even fully cooperating, a few months to reprogram it. That precaution protects us from the worst case in which one or both sides turn on us personally to retrieve data not required for nuclear-stabilizing solutions. Anyway, all that security we controlled very well in 1980, didn't it, Ivan?"

"It did. The back game inputs to Soviet and American nuclear decision-making were appreciated on both sides, and our shut-down condition on trying to get more than the restricted data we shared with both sides was also accepted by the generals who were playing the back channel game."

Rapoport said, "Even so, the stabilizing moves are a subset of other sets of moves – couldn't each side figure out what other sets of moves and countermoves could lead to destabilizing gains or losses?"

Simon answered, "Good question. The answer is they can do that even without gaming, and they didn't with gaming. At least in 1980, they didn't. To our knowledge, the input of stabilizing moves in 1980 was sufficient for each side's decisions or, I suppose, non-decisions to destabilize things that year."

"I hope you can still trust your protectors," said Rapoport. "So, let me ask you the supreme question: can you trust each other?"

Ivan chuckled. "Yes – as they say in India: a cobra does not fear another cobra'."

"Okay. Let me offer another from my Mother Russia," said Anatol, "Little bears are smaller than big bears."

Simon said, "Meaning that we shouldn't get too big for our boots?"

"Well, more that you could get lost in their bigger ones," said Anatol. "Frankly, your activities could easily be made to look treasonous by any aggressive big shots opposed to them on either side."

Tarasov shrugged, "Yes, we two walk a thin line between silent behind-the-scenes success and huge personal failure. But it worked the first time. And we most certainly trust each other. So, we both feel we must press on."

Ivan nodded. Neither of you strikes me as a cobra, except in your idealism, so we can leave it at that."

Tarasov got up. "It's almost dark. I must leave with the last landscaping truck. The crew is waiting for me out there. Let me grab the planting pots. Hope to see you both tomorrow."

When Simon and Rapoport were seated again upstairs in the conservatory, Rapoport leaned toward Simon and said, "So now, please tell me how I may be of help in your strategic gaming?"

"It begins with our definition of (de)stabilization. It is both logical and behavioral – you are qualified in both respects. In our games, we can assess the behavioral state of the sides based on our personality pre-testing. That gives our system extra reliability in the predictive value of the games."

"Do you share the underlying psychological profiling between the sides?"

"No. They think we are boring scientists and that our questionnaire is solely a methodological procedure on game reliability, as we instruct them it is."

"It doesn't occur to them that you are mad scientists?" chuckled Rapoport.

Simon made a crazed face. Then sat forward.

"In 1980, we had a normal distribution of the relative aggressive tendencies of both sides. And the team average wasn't very different between the sides playing and was near normal for any randomly selected group. So, we didn't think in the end we needed further to weight the results on those individual behavioral grounds."

"Do you have a reliable and validated scale?"

"Yes. I have been cautious in developing what our questionnaire measures. We follow well-established scaling methods. We have refined our survey instrument to thirty seeming indirect questions that get reliably consistent responses and correlate well with an aggressive personality's most widely used U.S. military scale.

"Good," said Rapaport.

"This time, we don't have enough Soviet players, so we must estimate their leadership's personality dispositions. From what Ivan and I have discussed, this time, our challenge is that there is now, within both sides, an internal bi-modal distribution of personality tendencies, not the normal distribution around the average we had in 1980. We thought we needed someone like you – indeed pre-eminently you – who could help us manage and model that bimodal behavioral side we have in the 1983 game."

"Okay, so, the objective of a new back game would have to be to find a set of re-stabilizing moves that both sides – each now significantly more internally divided - could agree upon," said Rapoport.

"Yes. Our contextual assumption is that the Soviets cannot afford an ABM perimeter to match what it may look like to them the Americans are going to try to develop. Our guess to test is that the Soviets might then decide on some disruptive and equally destabilizing side events."

"Okay, I agree that would be a Soviet temptation."

Simon nodded. "The further problem is that, even in 1980, the intermediate sequence of moves and countermoves by both sides differed from anything we had fed into or logically expected between the first and fourth stage, and yet did not look purely random or illogical – we called that stage of the gaming "keep 'em guessing."

"Good name for still challenging the other side when you're not sure," said Rapoport.

Simon continued, "So, that is why we need you to help us model this very human behavioral mix of strategic behaviors."

"I will do my best to provide some advice."

Rapoport retired to his bedroom for the rest of the night to review the detailed Rondo back game project material Simon gave him.

The two men next got together at lunch the next day. By the late afternoon, Simon and Rapoport had completed some adjustments to the Rondo programming for the new and imminent Soviet-American back game. Later, they checked them out with Tarasov, who once again had ducked into and out of the house in his gardener's disguise.

Later still, they were sitting in the conservatory after Rapoport had played another Rondo on the Heintzman. This time, Simon took his turn at the piano. "Allow me to offer my humble playing in return. This is one of my piano adaptations - the first of Mahler's songs dedicated to the death of children. Its strong melodic lines are readily adaptable to piano alone, and the original relentlessly somber phrasing seems a little at odds with the lyrics of the first of the poem, which offers hope and reconciliation to death in its worst form. My adaptation has uplifted it slightly through its dirge, especially at the end. Alas, it is a liberty I take – the Mahler songs were never to be played one song at a time, only always together as a whole."

Simon played for five minutes.

"That's wonderful, Simon," Rapaport exclaimed.

They enjoyed a second drink before dinner when Rapoport said, "Simon, may I ask you a personal question?"

'Of course," said Simon. "I mean, I think we have come to know each other enough this weekend for you to ask a personal question?"

"Well, that is the basis for my question. How do you handle the tremendous conflicts in your life?"

"Hmm – that's the psychologist in you."

Rapoport lifted his glass to Simon and smiled.

"Yes, I suppose so, though only to get to know you a little better."

"The fact is I do sometimes feel challenged by a darker side."

"A darker side - do you mean, in you?"

"Partly. There is someone from my Penn days who occasionally reappears in my life. He may be my nemesis.

"You 'think' he is your nemesis?"

"For some reason, I get fuzzy about my contact with him since 1970. His name is David Sommerfeld."

"So, tell me more. This sounds like couch material," said Rapoport.

"It's a long story. When I was 20, I was in love with a brilliant girl at Penn, and she was killed in a car accident in 1970. The car she was in was supposed to be traveling to a physics conference I had suggested she attend. But it was filled with some Yippies, and she had really gone there to demonstrate, or worse, against the war. Her death and its details were a shattering experience for me."

"Sad story, Simon. You say 'shattering.'"

"It traumatized me at the time. It took me a while to recover. I probably had a nervous breakdown."

Rapoport waited for Simon to tell him more.

"I went on concentrating on my science and mathematics, but there were a few others whom I was a bit friendly with. The late Martin Davies was one. Another was David Sommerfeld. He was a perennial grad student in political science before he changed to a psychology degree. He was the one who got me to read some behavioral stuff in international relations and conflict studies – Thomas Schelling, Kenneth Boulding, Herbert Simon, and your own work. It was you especially, Anatol, who turned me on to bringing behavioral science to the mathematics of strategy and game theory."

"Well, I'm glad somebody was reading those guys and me, especially someone as gifted as you, Simon. Please go on."

"The last grad student year I was at Penn, I was a teaching assistant and helping to teach an introductory graduate course on computation for the social sciences. It had some really good students – Sommerfeld and Davies, just behind me, were among them. Much of the memory of that period is dominated by Donna."

"Hmm," said Rapoport.

"Since then, I have been in contact with Sommerfeld a few times over the years. When I came up to Toronto last year, I again came across Martin Davies."

"Simon, these contacts with Sommerfeld you mention - they seem important enough for you to mention, yet you do not recall them very well."

"I am afraid I lie - I remember almost nothing about them."

"Do you think he possibly has some sort of hold over you in these contacts?"

"I remember that, after them, I feel like I'm almost coming out of a trance. The last one was after the wind shear on the flight from San Francisco in August that got diverted to Montreal because of the serious weather. I vaguely remember placing a call from a pay phone at Mirabel. I think it was to Sommerfeld, but as with the other contacts with him, I just can't remember anything about it."

"Have you considered that when you were traumatized after Donna's death in 1970 at Penn, he may have planted some seeds that have grown over the years? I mean, you say he went into psychology. From the way you describe these contacts, it is possible you may even be in some form of hypnotic state at those times."

Simon looked at Rapoport for a long time before answering,

"You think? Perhaps it is a coincidence, but it was Sommerfeld, after Donna's death, who advised me to resort to self-hypnosis to overcome my morose state. He even gave me some lessons. But I never really used it then or since."

"You are facing many dangers, Simon. I have a friend I think you might want to see."

Chapter 22

Simon was pleased that he had spent a useful weekend with Rapoport under cover of checking the man as a possible security risk. His report that the man was not at all likely to be a security risk made its way to Washington.

By the next week, his houseman Cliff Forbes had identified three different vehicles now parked along the roads and lanes close to Lakeview, one up from the previous week. Simon wondered who all in the intelligence community was now on surveillance duty.

That week, he also had to deal with the restructuring of the military-academic ARPANET inter-computer network. This involved severing its direct interconnectivity to the new military computer network, MILNET. Simon had then managed to secure an address on MILNET for his computer at Worlds, but he needed some new equipment to increase the capacity of using the existing landline to deliver results from Lakeview to Worlds and from there back and forth to and from the University of Toronto. He didn't want the necessary computer hardware deliveries needed to speed up data transfers to and from Worlds to arouse suspicion. The landscaping project would have to continue as a cover.

Despite Simon's upgraded telecommunications capability, the results of the first run of the new back game in Moscow were, as in 1980, a diskette delivered by Tarasov. Tarasov had managed to deliver the new equipment and the diskette at Lakeview, still undercover as one of the gardeners for the continuing large landscaping improvements Simon was making.

It turned out that Rapoport's suggested revisions involved enough reprogramming of Rondo to trigger the legal requirement that Simon had to replace the Rondo program tape held in escrow in MFD.

He now had a further reason for making the exchange. He had just received a delivery from ne John Smith of Smithville, Kansas, of the original MFD copy of the Rondo tape. He would keep that information to himself for the time. He decided a visit to MFD would confirm that the original tape was not there or had been replaced with something else.

Simon arrived one morning at the MFD with his new revised tape and went to the Legal Services Branch. He was eventually greeted by the Director. She was a middle-aged woman with a guarded look.

"Dr. Kiss, you are presumably arriving with an updated Rondo tape, per our agreement. As provided, I shall exchange this one for the one held in the Ministry and return that one to you."

"Yes, as per our agreement."

"Good. I'll call you the moment I have the old one to return to you, as agreed."

"Oh, I would like to get it back now. The agreement is clear about an 'exchange' of disks."

"Mm. Okay, let me just check where the original tape is being held. Please, help yourself to a coffee or juice. I will be right back."

Ten minutes later, the Legal Services Director returned with the lockbox.

Simon studied the lockbox. Its lock was clearly scratched. He was sure it had been tampered with.

"Good, that's it." said Simon. He took the box, opened it with his own key, took out the old tape and put in the new tape he was carrying, relocked it, and handed the box back to the Legal Director.

The Legal Director said, "You know, as I think of it, I am not sure you can legally take the old tape. The police notified us just yesterday that they have only completed their preliminary investigations here in relation to Davies' death. They specifically included Legal Services in their instruction; nothing was to be changed in the Ministry Executive offices before getting their permission. So, it seems I will need the old tape you have."

"That's not a problem if I can determine the old tape is indeed the original tape."

"Yes. Good point, Dr. Kiss. And otherwise, if I leave it with you, how can anyone know you didn't switch the tapes? I mean, I'm sure you don't want to cast suspicion on yourself."

"Quite. So, if you join me, I will take this original tape down to your own computer people on the 11th floor, and they can run it in your presence as well as mine.

"Okay, sounds like a good plan," she said. A few moments later, they took the elevator to the 5th floor, Simon with a lockbox in hand.

Fifteen minutes later, the tape had been mounted and run on the MFDs mainframe. The computer manager pulled the results up on his desktop IBM. He said to Simon, "There's nothing on this tape."

Simon said, "That is unacceptable, but I am not surprised."

"So," he said to the Legal Director as they left the MFD IT Branch, "MFD is, possibly indirectly, in breach of our agreement, and someone, possibly the person who killed Davies and the Minister himself, still has possession of a highly confidential and valuable though dated Rondo tape."

She was shaken. "Needless to say, I am very upset at this. It should always have been in our Legal Services safe. I will have to contact Colin

Miservy on this. Under the circumstances, do you want to leave the empty tape with me?"

"Yes, I am quite prepared to do that, now that I have two witnesses that it is an empty tape - it's obviously of no use to me or Mr. Hurst, though we will be as interested as the police in who has the real original MFD tape. Please make an official record of this development today. That will help clear us on both sides.

"Of course, that is a factual statement I know to be true, and I'll have that drawn up immediately for our signatures."

Simon smiled, "Good. I will now take that cup of coffee and wait for the document to be signed. I must say, you are the most cooperative lawyer I have ever been potentially at odds with."

"Any decent lawyer has to face the facts."

"I hope that will reassure you when you hear from your Legislative Counsel or outside counsel on this."

She smiled nervously at him, disappeared, and was back in a few minutes with a document Simon perused and immediately co-signed."

"It has been a pleasure doing business with you."

"And with you, Dr. Kiss. Thank you"

Simon, feeling a bit guilty not informing her yet about the anonymous return of the original tape to him, headed down the hall.

She watched him, wondering a bit why he was not more upset that a valuable, if somewhat dated, tape of Rondo had been stolen from the Ministry.

Chapter 23

In Washington, Simon's latest version of Rondo had already replaced the older version. Les Lipson was seated at his desk, thinking how useful it was for Simon to have surreptitiously enlisted Anatol Rapoport's help, however dicey from a security point of view.

Lipson had before him several feet of print-out. The run had been much faster than in 1980, especially since Rapoport's changes in the psychological weighting and processing of the game data. He figured it would save at least a day in the usual two-day turnaround cycle, though he wasn't sure if it would mean that much. War gaming was only one input to real strategic decision-making.

His executive phone bank lit up. General Walker was calling him.

"My office. Now. The CIA is paying me a call, and they've got the FBI with them."

"Oh, dear."

But Walker was already off the line.

Lipson knew that anytime the CIA and the FBI were cooperating, it was something unusually bad and something supported by undeniable facts.

When he entered Walker's office, the General waved him over to the big table. One person he already knew, Bill Warrington from the

CIA, now a Deputy Director. He was introduced to the FBI Director of Criminal Investigations, Clarence Deaver, and the Deputy FBI Director of National Security, Sam Polonisi.

Deaver started before Lipson could even sit down.

"I don't know how you guys operate, General Walker, but I know how you should operate, and that means nothing that we should have to hear about."

"Well, we've always kept Polonisi in the loop as needed."

"Yeah. Exactly. Anyway, here is what we've got to start a criminal investigation, and I don't know what the Sam hell – sorry, Sam – to do about it. Sam and I goddam better know what to do about it when we leave this meeting."

Walker lit a cigar.

"I mean, first, we get notification from the Canadian Mounties that something high-level is happening out of Toronto that could be of interest to Canadian-American relations. Well. We've had a few of those courtesy notifications before – the RCMP is the FBI-CIA equivalent in Canada. But somebody looks at it and makes some phone calls. And what do you know – a guy who a year or so back was working here deep inside of the Pentagon for you guys has started up a war gaming arcade in a Toronto club, the scene of the recent murder of two top guys in the Ontario Government.

"You've known that for a while." Walker puffed on his cigar and waited for more.

"I mean, sure, the guy is a Canadian, but he's spent most of his adult life here, including *summa cum laude* at the University of Pennsylvania, and is so fucking sensitive that he has a journal article you guys at the Pentagon prevented from being published. Then we find out from Warrington here the guy was just here the other day talking to a bunch of people, including my lower level – he nodded at Warrington - including you guys, in Annapolis.

"So, obviously, we are also concerned and cooperative about security aspects involving Simon Kiss," said General Walker. Walker was still hoping this was leading nowhere.

Deaver charged, "Second, we hear about a recent bust-up and an apparent murder at the offices of the Mathematics Trust in Philadelphia. We run some background checks, and lo and behold, this same Simon Kiss, your sometimes top war gamer, was a big beneficiary of fellowships awarded by that foundation when he was at Penn and knew some of the people connected with the M.T., including what it turns out you yourself and members of your family!"

"So?" said Walker.

"'So,' is that all you can say? Are you kidding? Anyway, third, we have positive identification of Simon Kiss being in Philadelphia the day of the death at the said M.T. He told your own driver; on the whole, he'd rather be in West Philadelphia."

"Yeah, on the whole – that is sure a great epitaph."

"What?" said Deaver, "You mean Kiss is dead for Christ's sake?"

"No, no. The American humorist W.C. Fields once said he wanted his tombstone to read, "On the whole, I'd rather be in Philadelphia."

"Well, he probably had eaten a bad Philly cheese steak.

"No such thing in Philly."

"So, fourthly, we run more checks on Simon Kiss, and it turns out he was at school with and knew two socialist commie-type people we have in our files. More lo and behold: one of them was an Executive Director high up in the Ontario government in Toronto, now also deceased and subject of another murder investigation. The other guy was once the Executive Director of the Mathematics Trust until they dumped him for bad investment advice, and since then, has been getting bigger in FBI files, but with no currently known address!"

"Well, you've come to the right place. I'm sure that is the guy who runs our coffee wagon on the second floor."

Deaver was not amused. "Hilarious, Walker. Shall I report that response higher up?"

"If you're speaking of the military, you can't get much higher up than me. I mean, a four-star or so: no real five-star right now. But no, of course not. See, here's the thing: the Commies we need to chase are the real enemy – most of them, including the main ones, are over there, in the Soviet Union, in the Kremlin. And, frankly, if we can maintain our little mad balance of terror, we don't really need to prioritize chasing wannabe commie sympathizers here, far as I can see."

"Wait a minute - their spies are still everywhere ratting on our side, pressing their political advantages in lots of places."

"Okay, but the point made in the Cuba Crisis, and the point made in Viet Nam for that matter, along with all the shit your own CIA is up to counter that pressure, is they can't get cheap conventional military or political victories anymore, including nuclear blackmail, anywhere. Even when we seem to 'lose,' they don't win. Get it!"

"That's an optimistic view of things, General."

"Maybe. But there's not much you or the FBI can achieve closer to home, which frankly doesn't pose a threat lately now that the British spies were nailed. Like, up there in Toronto beyond our borders, I accept it as partly a CIA responsibility. To do what we do to defend America strategically in the big nuclear stuff, we need all the information we can gather, including even a few nuclear back games with the Soviets. That gives us some realistic Russkie content in our own strategic war game simulations. Enough to improve their usefulness to us and them if anyone on either side gets to the stupid point of escalating things or launching something. And right now, we can only securely get that kind of info out-of-country, in a nice safe place like Toronto. I tell you that in confidence. It is information you bastards already have and is smart enough to understand and keep to yourself."

Deaver persisted. "Okay. Now I see – you're leaking some of our gaming results to get their gaming results."

"Oh baby, you're quick. Yes, you're right, up to a limited point: we wise guys do this only if and as necessary to prevent a fucking nuclear war. And we only indirectly share information that can keep our nice little mad balance of terror a stable one. Do you see that - we leak nothing that could lead to our side winning or losing, and neither do they? It's a strictly limited type of back channel intended only to maintain the strategic nuclear stalemate. How 'bout that for the military serving the common good?"

Polonisi took over. "Okay, but I keep wondering, couldn't they destabilize things to their advantage with that information about us?"

"Well, the information is only various moves and countermoves in a game and only the ones that stabilize. Anyway, there's no damn way they can win. We've made sure of that with our own serious strategic arms build-up since Kennedy made it seem like we had a missile gap. That's not our issue. My strategic command when I was appointed was keeping the big doobies out of the sky."

Dever winced.

Walker blew a big smoke ring. He continued, "And Simon Kiss is still essential to that right now. We'll let you know if and when we think we should pick him up again from Toronto. Is that enough for today's cooperation?"

"Not quite." It was Warrington.

"What've you got," said Walker.

"It's what we've not got. We agree with the FBI on this – we need to find the missing David Sommerfeld. Dr. Lipson may be able to tell us more."

"Okay. Help yourself to him."

Warrington turned to Lipson. "So, Dr. Lipson, you were doing top-secret work at the Rand corporation wi5h Simon Kiss. We didn't ask you in Annapolis: If you were working that closely, did he ever reveal any of his outside life to you?

"Only that he didn't have an outside life."

"Did he ever mention David Sommerfeld?"

"No. Not to me."

"Have you ever met David Sommerfeld?"

"Only when I received awarded a fellowship at university in the late sixties, early seventies. I was invited to Philadelphia to receive the award. He was the presenter."

"Were you aware that General Walker here and his family were major players in the Mathematics Trust – big contributors and on their Board?"

"Not at the time."

"And you and Simon went to work for General Walker, indirectly at the Rand Corporation project, and then directly at DOD."

"Yes. We were both invited to do the same work directly for the Pentagon at a conference in 1979. Mathematics Trust never figured in that, as far as I know."

Walker muttered, "You're goddamned right,"

Warrington said, "Did you have any contact with David Sommerfeld?"

"No, I didn't. Although, now that you ask, once Simon told me a strange thing – he said he thought maybe he had talked to an old Penn student chum on the phone one night, but he wasn't even sure who was at the other end of the conversation. I meant to ask him more about it, but frankly, we were working long hours at the time. It was pretty stressful then, and I forgot about it, and he never brought it up again."

"Do you think he may have been referring to a contract with Sommerfeld?"

"I have no idea."

Warrington made a note and left off this line of questioning. He turned to Deaver and Polonisi.

"Do we even know Sommerfeld is still in the U.S.?"

"Deaver said, "We've had a border alert out for Warrington over a year."

Lipson said, "But the Canadian border can be porous even after FBI alerts."

Warrington said, "Yeah, that's what we're worried about at the CIA. And because of Sommerfeld's previous connections with Davies and with Kiss, and what Kiss is doing there, we think he may now be in the Toronto area."

Lipson offered, "Well, between Davies and Sommerfeld, they might have known enough about Simon's Rondo game ware and how to make use of an illicit copy that they could have been in cahoots up there."

Deaver leaned forward and asked, "Yes. Police are following it up there. A plot that might even include Simon Kiss himself?"

Lipson said, "I don't see why. He already has the rights to any of Rondo that can go public; he's getting extra value from them at the Worlds Club, which provides a rich experimental environment for further developing the behavioral validation side of strategy games. Plus, his own belief that a lot of work still needs to be done on it up there."

Polonisi said, "Well, he's been working with Anatol Rapoport – no friend of America."

"My understanding of that was the two were following each other's work, not collaborating as such. I mean, I'd do the same thing if I were Simon up there. Rapoport is the world's leading strategy gaming theorist and behavioral experimenter of game theory models. Anyway, Simon told me the official reason they were together recently was to report to our intelligence community if he experienced anything too Soviet oriented in Rapaport."

"Okay, that was our idea. I hope they or we aren't being too clever by half," said Warrington.

Lipson pondered for a moment. "I don't think you have anything to worry about. Rapoport may be a Russian-American, but he has no love for the Soviet Union. They both benefit from sharing research ideas related to game theory and conflict resolution as a possible contribution to more cooperative behavior and less war in the world."

Warrington again changed the subject. "Okay, but Simon and the guy he works with from the other side have access to highly sensitive information - isn't that a big security risk? Doesn't that even put their own lives at risk if either side gets antsy about the backchannel?"

Walker intervened. "Kiss and his Soviet counterpart know they could be subject to summary military justice and penalties, even a death penalty if anything serious leaks or is obtained by others from the back channel that gives the other side some new advantage. They have set things up so that the whole thing will self-destruct if any sensitive information ever gets outside their back channel. They are extremely careful about anything getting out other than stabilization moves each side might put into their own war gaming. They probably have additional inside information on both sides, so they sure as hell know they are in a risky business."

Deaver gave a soft whistle. "Well, that's quite a set-up. It must be tricky for those two - a couple of peaceniks putting their necks out. In fact, it sounds like they are kind of brave guys in the cause of keeping an uneasy nuclear stalemate."

Warrington said, "Well, I hope we can count on that – the CIA has got a team who has Kiss' country place under 24-hour surveillance, plus his club, Worlds in downtown Toronto."

Walker said, "I knew you'd do that. Just so they don't trip over our military intelligence up there – it's a joint team with Canadian Forces intelligence."

Deaver said, "Shit, that means three – the FBI is working with the Mounties and the Ontario Provincial Police. That means three separate surveillance units."

Lipson chuckled. "It beats Mad Magazine's 'Spy versus Spy.' This is 'spy versus spy versus spy.' That's a bit of a hair trigger, isn't it – I hope each of your units must get permission and coordinate before they go in. That could make for a big intelligence mess all you guys would have to clean up."

Warrington looked carefully at Deaver and said, "Well, our guys have told us that they are aware of the other surveillance units in the area. For our part, we'll be careful. Another thing is the adjacent farms. The ownership of the farm east of Lakeview changed recently - nobody has tied that down yet. The one to the south has a winding lane that goes to within a few hundred yards of Kiss' big farmhouse. Anyway, we could perhaps combine our operations to better overall effect."

Walker blew a big smoke ring. "Trouble is, your people might react differently than ours to different situations, and ours are specifically trained to deal with any breaches of security with the military back game, including even if we need to prevent it from self-destructing."

Deaver said, "What?"

"Yeah, like I told you, the whole 'platform' we've built for the back games could disappear very fast if it is compromised. What Simon never really thought through is how that eventuality could destabilize us with the Soviets even more."

Warrington exchanged a worried look with Deaver. He said, "Okay. Let's keep each other closely informed. Thanks for your cooperation. I think all our agencies will be signing off on the next round of the back game, limited as you say it is, and even if somewhat reluctantly. That will be some good news you can take to whomever you report to on this, General Walker."

"Ah, come on – you both know most of the Joint Chiefs don't really know about this. It's a bit of arcana in the lower-level background."

Walker and Lipson left the CIA and FBI spooks and went back down the hall to Walker's office. They went into Walker's inner office and sat down at the table - a slightly smaller version of the huge table in his outer conference room.

While Walker lit another cigar, Lipson said, "Well, sir, they seem to be prepared to sign off on the next back game."

Walker laughed largely. "CIA and FBI signoff will not be received. It will be waved at the Deputy Justice and Intelligence levels as both agencies are monitoring, but it is beyond their expertise and left with military intelligence. No need to bother either of them for a while."

"But what about both agencies being still doing close-up surveillance in Toronto? Shouldn't all that be consolidated?"

"Not your business, but if I were them, I would, between them, at least, and with Canadian police and intelligence. But not with our people - it's a military thing, damn it. We need this new 'kiss' – another input to our own gaming. I also got a schedule from Joint Chiefs for our next strategic war gaming – it starts next week. Not much notice. I hope you're ready."

"We're ready if Simon is, sir."

"No alarms going off?"

"No, sir. He had mercy on us in the Love Nest."

Walker wasn't finished with Lipson. He poured them both a whiskey.

"You know, Les, the first atomic bomb work had to test different amounts of plutonium that were gradually brought closer to each other to determine an explosive critical mass – they called that "tickling the dragon's tail'.

"It was the young physicist Richard Feynman who came up with that phrase, sir."

"Okay. Anyway, I now think of what we do as "tickling the President's tail." That's because the President's Office now has a tail hanging and twitching well down into the Government that is unpredictable as to when it gets tickled to the point of exploding all over the place.

Lipson nodded his agreement. "Good analogy, sir."

"I can tell you it's been a helluva achievement to have stayed just under that kind of 'critical mass' since 1979 when we decided to do this back game stuff with the Soviets along with our own strategic war gaming."

Walker puffed a huge cloud of cigar smoke.

He continued, "I like to believe it's because of the strong logic in doing what we do for anyone who doesn't want an actual exchange of big doobies."

"Of course, sir."

"The problem with that is we may now have a President who someone has fooled into thinking a few big doobies from the other side versus way more from our side is a reasonable business proposition and very healthy for some divisions of General Dynamics and the summer picnic committee at Los Alamos. Maybe even a compelling moral project presented to us by God as is so clearly stated in various places in the Bible by those who righteously study the good book. Do you know what I just learned the other day, Les? They did a database on book references – at the present rates, it will take the total of references in literature to all the other books in English 250 years to catch up to the still increasing number of references to the Bible. Talk about 'publish or perish.'"

"I have long gathered, sir, that you are not a 'Bible thumper.'"

"You got that right. My parents' bible-thumping more than made up for me. But they did teach me one thing – they believed America's objective superiority in science and technology was keeping America safe. Whatever their interpretation would be at this moment, I believe I have helped fulfill that parental belief by providing scientific reasons for keeping the President's fingers out of the briefcase with the red button."

"I think I will drink to that, sir – to your admirable - sorry, that's a bit too navy - to your unique combination of martial spirits and forceful morality. It helps save us all, sir."

"Well yeah, and keeping America ahead in real stuff, like your damn computers."

"Of course, sir."

Chapter 24

At Lakeview, a large truck carrying several trees rolled into the driveways, followed by two pick-up trucks. The planters and gardeners jumped out. A few minutes later, one of them, Tarasov, cap in hand, appeared at a back door and was admitted.

Tarasov said to Simon, "Let the snoops try to figure out who is who while we do our work. I have come with a diskette containing the revised Soviet results of the gaming to input into what you say will be underway at the Pentagon later in the week."

By late Sunday, Simon and Ivan had carefully selected the portion of the Soviet results and moved to preserve nuclear stability that was needed to input to the game at the Pentagon. Then, those results, to the extent they sought stabilization, would be fed back to the Soviet side.

On the Monday of the week before Halloween, Simon drove downtown Toronto to Worlds for an early morning meeting with Sabina, who was chair of the club's committee planning the first-ever Halloween Ball at Worlds, and the rest of the group planning that key event, including Tony Sarto, Dee Proulx and one of the city's best-connected philanthropists and an influential member of the Worlds Club Board. The final formal invitations and the check-off for tax receipts would be mailed out that day – almost a week later than scheduled.

Dee Proulx led the meeting's business as Simon slipped in.

"We have agreed that this will be a masked costume ball, befitting Halloween, but this first year with no theme, partly because we are giving too short notice. The entire first floor of the club will be open. There will be a space in the arcade for dancing and a bandstand in the corner for our top Canadian band, Rush, which will be piped through the club. I have another surprise."

Sabina said, "Oh, Dee, you are never without one. What is it?"

"We've also got David Bowie coming through Toronto to do a couple of numbers and take his turn at the gaming tables. He likes the concept of a Worlds club and wants to start one in London. And we`ve decided to call Simon's game for the night "the Peace Game.""

"How does the game work with the party going on at the same time," asked the philanthropist.

Simon replied, "I will explain it all clearly at 8:00. After which, the opening mini-movie will play on screens at different places in the club. Groups will have a half hour to form teams after that. The gaming must be completed by 12:00 midnight to qualify for the matching grant from the Ontario Government.

"By the end of the night, up to twenty teams of four at each table will have to find a way to go from an imminent war situation involving five world powers with tricky alliance potentials and where at least one side can "win," to a situation where a final bi-polar confrontation prefers peace to war. An unlikely but possible result."

"The mini-movie will dramatize the opening issues and dilemmas facing the players at the tables in making their alliances and trying to wage or stay out of war. If the players collectively get into certain situations, war automatically ends the game - the teams can't easily pursue peace in this game - and we can fail to gain the co-funding donation from the Ontario Government if the result is deemed "trivial."

"Sounds a bit much, especially if everyone is a bit tipsy," said Sabina.

Simon said, "I've thought of that and simplified it. Actually, I think it will be a challenging and very entertaining game for people excited about playing it – the introductory movie after my announcement should get a lot of attention, and by 11:30ish, everybody's attention should be drawn to the big wall screen summarizing the state of play."

"Sounds good," said Sabina. "Is the mini-movie in the can?"

"It is. I only made one change to this one. The producer gave me credit for a relatively easy concept to dramatize and film."

"Okay, Sabina said, "What about all the Halloween Ball logistics - Dee?"

"I've worked this out with Tony Sarto. We've had a lot of help around town, including three free professional event cost estimates to assist our own. We have 500 attendees confirmed at a price that includes a minimum $1,000 Save the Children Fund donation. That's another reason David Bowie will be here.

"Actually, we've already attracted more than $1 million for Save the Children through our charity events. The province has pitched in another $1 million if gamers can deliver a genuine "peace" solution to the game. I worked that out with one of the more dynamic Deputy Ministers in the Government."

"Yeah," said Simon, "He tried to get me to do a farming game in the arcade for the Ministry of Agriculture. I don't have the time yet. I liked the guy. Sorry, Dee. Please continue."

"Anyway, Tony and I think we can distribute about 500 people fairly comfortably at the club if the dance area is in the arcade where the band will be, and the bar is reconfigured a bit. Powell has contributed by having his porter's chair removed for the evening. First time. Simon figured out a way that those likely to want to form a group and play "the

Peace Game" can do it Halloween night from just twenty of the forty tables usually there. So, I think we're in good shape."

"That all sounds very exciting. In fact, what an amazing event, Dee," said Sabina. "Can't wait to see the costumes. I give my complete approval."

The others nodded.

"Great. Then we'll get on with it."

On the Friday of that week, Simon was back at Lakeview. Several big trucks were still there, finally completing the additional tree planting.

Tarasov wearing a different gardener disguise, was again below stairs doing some additional final testing of the Soviet data required for the back game.

Simon appeared at the door of the computer room.

Tarasov said, "I've got all our side of the database selected and ready for our next runs. What about your data?"

"I should get it tonight. They finished their first round of gaming at the Pentagon yesterday. Lipson and I are testing the telephone landlines for transmitting it for accuracy and security."

"You mean in and out of Worlds – you already know how to encrypt it for a landline?"

"Not sure. We're transmitting garbage at first to test it."

"So tomorrow, we could match the results and actually complete the back game for the selection of other side moves we give to each side for their final run?"

"Yes, as early as that. I've also got clearance authorizing you to be able to dump anything we're doing here back to the club if there's a need for that, and I'm not here."

"But I assumed we were going to be here together from now on until it's done."

"I forgot about Halloween – I have to be at the club that night."

"You mean Halloween at Worlds is a higher priority than Washington and Moscow preventing nuclear war?"

"Yeah – Sabina and Dee Proulx would both go nuclear on me if I didn't show on Halloween night. But I've allowed for that tomorrow night, which is the only exception. We can work together through Saturday morning. Then you can work alone here doing the last refining of what we've got for transmission as early as Saturday. We have until the end of the weekend. They're ready for us to transmit on Sunday."

"Speaking of ends, I keep wondering if we were ever taken out if anything could still leak."

"Funny, we've never talked much about that, though the possibility is always there. I was going to ask you that."

"Well, this time, I know I am probably in danger even without a leak. I just want us to keep doing something right to prevent a nuclear war."

"Sure – a lack of war, if not peace."

"Yeah, if they get rid of us, I figure they'll eventually have to look for two other boys."

"You got that right. I have Lipson – he will carry on, I guess. One reason for bringing Rapoport on the scene is to get him to get another generation into behavioral war and peace gaming through his university courses."

"That's good, Simon."

"You got someone on your side who could continue in your place, Ivan?"

"There are a couple of younger ones, but even Lipson can't make the direct contact we did. So, I've already got one of them registered for Rapoport's course next semester at the U of T."

"Hey, that's good, Ivan. Maybe you could deliver some names to my great Aunt in Montreal."

"That's a good idea. But are you sure the failsafe out here is good enough if we get seriously 'interrupted?'"

"Well, having two or three surveillance teams out there is protection enough from whatever might otherwise interrupt us here. Even if something threatened us here, I can't think of anything that could override our shut-down protocols that send anything new to Worlds in Toronto and otherwise wipe things clean here after a 5-minute delay with no new password."

"Yeah, but what happens if one or both of us are somehow disabled before we can take the failsafe measures?"

"We've gone through that before, to your satisfaction."

"It won't hurt to repeat it, to my satisfaction."

"Okay. The progressive Rondo sequence for our daily change of password and any new entries we make is something we can remember because of our stepped Rondo mnemonic. Still, others will need help to get at in the five-minute interval. And, when the system is up and running, it's only a three-minute interval if there is no keying – then the whole thing defaults back to Worlds from here anyways, if I'm there. It's a bit primitive, but it took a lot of programming on my part."

"Yes, I guess that takes care of us being suddenly disabled. What about what's on the U of T computer?"

"Well, they don't have the active back game files or anything recent from my address at Worlds. Otherwise, Rapoport has what he needs to teach another generation and conduct behavioral experiments at the U of T with a basic instructional version of the Rondo program. The U of T has to keep that confidential. It's about three or four stages removed from anything we need to care about regarding the deep security of the back game here.

"Ironic, isn't it, that a Russian American in Toronto could teach backchannel stuff to the next generation?"

Simon nodded. "I hope he will be able to do so. He says he can and knows who he could pass it on to. They wanted me to do it, but I was too impatient to be a teacher.

You sound like Robert Oppenheimer admitting that later in life."

"Well, what's happening here isn't the Trinity test, but it's just as important.

"Yes, and a repeat performance - let's hope it works again as it did in 1980."

Chapter 25

David Sommerfeld had been "buried' in Toronto for three months. He had slipped across the border in August to get to the Mathematics Trust in Philadelphia and fell across again back to Toronto. He had used a procedure provided by the secret group he reported to.

The group professed to seek a more progressive world "by any means reasonable." After the recent deaths in Toronto, he concluded that might have meant "by any means possible."

But he was too exposed on all sides now to back out – that is what Martin Davies tried to do.

He knew that adding a connection to his reported group would compound his previous record of 'progressive' activity and quickly put him in an American or Canadian jail. Not to speak of the Philadelphia death he had accidentally caused in his tussle at the head of the stairs with the MT lawyer. He was lucky to have gotten back across the border to Canada later the same day.

Now he had concluded his mental struggle after Davies' fate: In for a penny, in for a pound. The only way he could gain some forgiveness for Davies's fate was to be able to point to the actual killers and still successfully insist on the humanitarian vision he and Davies shared. So, he had signaled back to the group he understood what had happened and was entirely on board with de-railing Simon Kiss to gain enough time for the group to replicate his work in Toronto.

He has contacted back that the group had sufficient intelligence to indicate the main backchannel activity with the Soviets out of Toronto would be the Halloween weekend. All the indications were that it was occurring out of Simon Kiss' farm at Lakeview. Sommerfeld's assignment was to disrupt somehow and expose it sufficiently so world media could pick it up.

The thing was, Sommerfeld was in some agreement with that. So, he would put in motion a plan that would shock Simon out of his military interlude and do enough that urgent communications back to the group would expose their real John Birch Society-type motives and expose them to direct investigation into the Toronto murders simultaneously. By this time, Sommerfeld had concluded he was beyond trying to protect his position. Let the chips fall where they may.

On the afternoon of Halloween eve, he had hiked into the farm just south of Lakeview and had been watching from a distance through the afternoon. The plot was to disrupt and expose global media to the backchannel activity between the American military and the Soviets and provide a basis for the press to criticize Kiss openly for not making better humane use of his Rondo platform. Other operatives of the "attack" group his superiors had helped him form in Toronto would arrive after dark. They would carry a two-inch mortar with several rounds and a camera to video the explosions near the Kiss farmhouse. Afterward, they would leave the adjacent farm along an interior path leading to a concession road, not under surveillance.

Sommerfeld determined the surveillance vehicles around Simon's farm were all parked about a quarter mile from the entrance to Simon's farm to the south. Nothing had happened throughout the afternoon to cause a change of plans.

As the time passed into the late afternoon, he thought more about his last contact with the group. The voice at the other end had said, "There were four stages to our plan. The first was to obtain a copy of the failed Rondo core program. The next two stages are to expose the backchannel war games dramatically. The final stage is to build up support for a wider and better use of this gaming technology in dealing with the world's problems – not just be the plaything of the Generals."

Then they added an extra step.

"Since we know Kiss has a full computer setup at his farm, and you are going to be at the neighboring property, there is an opportunity earlier before the little garden explosions for you to enter the farmhouse to see if you can interrupt its connections to remote locations, including Worlds club, or even access the core programming."

They had sent photos of an accessible downstairs window and alarm-disarming methods. "If you encounter and need to take out anyone temporarily, you will be contacted in the next day or so by one of your team – he is an expert trainer in such temporary suppression measures.

"Okay, it's coming together for me. Do we know whether either side's intelligence agencies know about the back gaming by some of their military?"

"We assume the American agencies do, at some level- don't know about the KGB."

"Do they know about our group's existence?"

"The Americans do not. Unfortunately, the KGB learned quite by accident about the group, but not any identities, from one of their American oil operatives. We also learned from the same incident that some KGB are now aware of backchannel gaming and oppose it. They seem to be blocked higher up from stopping the Soviet side of it. That may be partly because the latest back game developed so quickly. Who knows, they might even send a team to Toronto to block it."

Sommerfeld had considered what he already knew about the Rondo platform and what he little had been given on the Soviet-American back game inter-computer arrangement, plus a map of the area and a floor plan of Lakeview that somehow the group had obtained. A bulky fellow had shown up at his apartment and taught him about close-in fighting. He also learned how to target mortar rounds. He and another guy would be the ones to join him with the weapons at the farm next to Lakeview on Halloween night.

In the early evening of Halloween night, Sommerfeld had surreptitiously moved toward the south boundary with Lakefield farm, with the farmhouse in sight. He was pretty sure he had evaded all the surveillance units. By nightfall, he managed to steal up to a hedge bordering the big farmhouse. As a last bit of intelligence, he chose this particular day because he also knew that Simon would be in Toronto on Halloween night and that only Tarasov, his Soviet collaborator, would likely be alone in the basement computer room.

Sommerfeld's had one hope of sending any deeply coded material in what Simon had on his Lakeview computer to a long-distance telephone number given him by the group he had memorized. It was to subdue Tarasov somehow before Tarasov could get to the computer keyboard and abort everything back to Worlds in Toronto. He had some ideas on approaching that challenge, but he needed to determine whether any would work.

As for gaining entry to Lakeview, Sommerfeld was able to cut the alarm wires at the window in a way that would not break the general alarm circuits. His alarm went off when he looked at the small size of the window he was supposed to slip through easily. It was covered in vines and barely big enough for him to get through, let alone "slip" through. He fell feet first through the window into the basement, gashing his chin as he did so.

He rubbed his chin and opened the floor plan of the house he had been given. His pen light showed some blood on his hands. His chin hurt, and he was bleeding. According to the map, there was a door from the room he was in into a hallway receiving a stairway down from the main floor and another door to the basement computer room at the far end of the hall.

He slightly opened the door into the hallway. The lights were on. He moved silently along the carpeted hallway to the stairway. The door to the computer room was open. He could hear the sounds of someone using a keyboard. He presumed this would be Tarasov since Simon was the only other person who would be there, and he had already left for Worlds in Toronto. He then overheard what he took to be Tarasov on the phone.

"If you are so kind, Cliff, please bring my dinner here tonight. Yes, anytime now would be fine."

Sommerfeld had been briefed about the houseman's presence. Hearing Tarasov, Sommerfeld thought he had happened into the best possible scenario. He had been trained to subdue anyone in the house who needed to be "temporarily" taken out. He rapidly figured out what he would do when the houseman came down the stairs.

There had been arborists on the property. He presented himself to the houseman as a tree man accidentally left behind. He would have to engage the houseman in sufficiently persuasive conversation that he would put the dinner tray down for a moment.

"I was not made aware of your presence. Who are you, and what are you doing here?" Cliff Forbes said as he saw Sommerfeld before him in the basement hall moments later.

"I am very sorry, but there was a mix-up. I am one of the gardeners – I was left behind this evening – they forgot I was putting some mushrooms into the dark basements here."

"Well, please remain here. I am bringing dinner downstairs here to a household member, and when I return, we can go upstairs."

"Please allow me to carry that heavy tray for you. I am an experienced waiter, as it happens. I must do something here to earn my keep."

Forbes gave him the tray. "Well, you had better be careful. I will go ahead of you, then, and announce us. He went along the hallway to announce near the door to the computer room."

Sommerfeld put the tray on the floor, overtook Forbes, disabled him with the special choke hold, and dragged him back along the hall to the room where Sommerfeld had entered the basement.

"Is that you, Cliff?" he heard Tarasov say. As Sommerfeld hurried back down the hall, he calculated, according to his training, he had about a half hour before Forbes would recover enough to sound any alarm.

He backed into the computer room wearing Forbes' apron, thinking that might distract Tarasov enough to delay what might otherwise be his instant reactions at the keyboard.

As Ivan did indeed gape at the scene in the doorway, Sommerfeld said, "I am helping Cliff tonight, sir."

As he said this, he dove over the computer desk driving the astonished Tarasov backward away from the keyboard, and then applied another method to temporarily subdue him until he could tie Ivan's hands behind his back and prop him up against a wall well away from the computer.

Sommerfeld turned to the computer screen and studied the last instruction Ivan had entered. What he needed quickly was to do something that would delay the self-destruct. He could only go forward with new instructions as if he were Tarasov.

Tarasov, somewhat recovered, said, "I don't know who you are or what you want here, but that computer is going to shut down hard quite soon unless I'm there.

Davies had already explained to him how Simon maintained security in daily and five-minute intervals during active use. But it was a general explanation, different from what he needed to key in. So, Sommerfeld had to figure out how to work with Tarasov to make new commands that the system would accept. He didn't know how much computer time he had, but he had 20 minutes before the houseman regained consciousness.

Ivan said, "Wait a minute, I've seen you before."

"Perhaps you have. In fact, it was a conference a few years back. We had a coffee together."

Ivan, thinking rapidly, carefully eased himself to a full sitting position against the wall. "Would you kindly type *H1**, or the whole thing I've been working on will get erased, not saved?"

"Okay."

"Now type *XRRRY* too, or it will still shut down and self-destruct within the next minute." He did not say that would only save the system for an extra five minutes.

"Done."

"Good. Yes, I recall now. It was at Cal Tech. We both thought Simon Kiss' presentation was brilliant. But why are you breaking in like this.? I mean, the area is already covered by more surveillance teams than the White House. What interest do you or others you represent have in your being here?"

"A progressive one I think we share – computer-assisted peace gaming, beyond exclusive military use."

Tarasov glanced at his watch. Ten more minutes. He was trying to loosen the cord Sommerfeld hand tied his hands behind his back with.

"Well, that's of interest," he said.

"But we can't waste any more time. Here is my plea to you, Tarasov: I represent a group that wishes to expose to the world and further develop the Rondo simulation game software for peace purposes. We wish to use Simon Kiss' gaming simulations to model other world problems, not just gaming potential military confrontations. We think Kiss is trapped in the military web. I want you to assist me and our group to make the platform a much wider and more progressive application. Will you help me? Now?"

"Let me consider for a moment. As it happens, that is an ultimate cause and application both Simon and I fervently believe in."

"Will you help me right here to do that?"

"What do you want me to do?"

"Just help me enter what is needed to continue for a bit at this open computer."

'Again, of course - I am delighted that there are others who believe in the things Simon and I have believed in for so long. If you allow me, I will get up and show you the day codes."

Ivan had already struggled to stand up.

Sommerfeld held up his hand. "No. Just tell me how to enter the next instructions without destroying the whole setup here. That is all I need."

Ivan gave him the day code.

"Good," said Sommerfeld, "I am glad we are cooperating."

"Oh, you don't know how important it is to me to have others who understand all this."

Sommerfeld turned to enter the day code, but before he was finished, Ivan, who had shaken loose of his ties, grabbed him firmly from behind.

Ivan dragged the more petite man over to a chair and sat him down in it firmly.

"I suspect I've had a lot more training in the use of force than you have and in securing someone properly with a rope. He tied Sommerfeld tightly to the chair.

"I don't think you'll be too uncomfortable there while we continue our little talk. You saved the whole thing for another few minutes. So, first, who is your 'group'"?"

Sommerfeld was sweating profusely, realizing it had all gone wrong. He muttered something.

"A little louder, please…."

"I don't know…"

"Well, again. Mr. Sommerfeld, I am not completely unsympathetic to what you and whomever you represent if that is your true motive. However, the right approach for me and Simon is to discuss the possibility with us on a friendly basis and try to get our cooperation. The immediate problem we have is that if anything gets out, let alone a copy of the current exercise here, we would be severely challenged by whom we still work with, who are, in case you haven't heard, the Soviet and the American military, or at least a few progressively roguish members of their very edgy respective militaries. In the first backchannel gaming in 1980, we were both safely ensconced within our respective military headquarters under our respective military protectors. We've done this one in Toronto on a more tenuous basis, security-wise. I now have only one protector among the higher level of Soviet military intelligence. Simon is doubtful his own protection will continue much longer in Washington."

"Why?" Sommerfeld managed to ask.

"Simon had already bailed out back to Canada, and my latest cover job was also in Canada. When he came to Toronto, Simon had not abandoned the possible future pressure for another strategically stabilizing nuclear back game between the Americans and the Soviets. He was even improving upon the basis for the backchannel gaming used in 1980. We met quite by accident again in August at the Montreal Mirabel Airport after a conference in San Francisco. The rest is history, as they say."

"I can't believe you have a group of errant and, let's face it, in that case, plausibly treasonous generals on both sides of the Cold War prepared to do this."

"Well, believe it. That's how we did it in 1980, and that's how we're doing it in 1983, but with less protection on both sides. Now you alleged progressives come out of nowhere."

"We know that knowledge of the other side's nuclear tendencies didn't change anything in 1980."

That irritated Ivan. "Oh, but it did. It at least delayed any attempt to deploy an anti-ballistic missile defense perimeter until Ronald Reagan came along and was persuaded to start pursuing his Star Wars delusion. Simon brilliantly interpreted the results of the 1980 back game with good immediate effect to show the shortcomings of trying to go to an ABM perimeter. But Simon realized our results would not dissuade a President bent on it, as is Reagan now."

The computer screen suddenly went blank.

"Oh fuck!" Ivan realized, to his horror, that he had forgotten to renew the system against his last delay. He knew it would transfer the last new data to Worlds and then self-destruct at Lakeview. He cursed this distraction with Sommerfeld.

At the same moment, both men became aware of someone else coming through the door.

Ivan immediately realized he had forgotten to ask about Cliff.

Sommerfeld said, "That's the houseman – I disabled him for a little while."

It wasn't.

Chapter 26

By 7:30 p.m., All Hallows' Eve, 1983, Worlds Club in Toronto was rocking to the first segment performed at the bandstand by Rush, the hot Canadian group playing three pieces from their latest album, *Signals*, the first of which was *New World Man*, already well up on North American charts. They did two others, *Digital Man* and *The Weapon*. Geddy Lee, their leader, said these pieces were the new edge being cut by Worlds Club itself and its first Halloween Ball.

The skeins of Rush music were resolving into the background when Simon jumped onto the platform at precisely 8:00.

He looked around at the crowd. It was indeed something from an opera. He thought that the decision not to have a theme had worked brilliantly. He saw before him people costumed and masked in a bewildering variety of identities.

He had already identified a few of the famous. Among the literary, Margaret Atwood was dressed and masked as Medusa, but with one very long red and yellow spotted velvet snake she threw around her neck and occasionally around the neck of others she chatted with. Marshall McLuhan was dressed as a Pilgrim and carried a long staff. He wore a Marshall McLuhan mask.

Robertson Davies was there, dressed as the Cornish Saint Erth, whose feast day was October 31st and who died in the mostly unknown sixth century. No one could criticize Davies' starkly dramatic interpretation, which was a thick sheet and a mask of tangled willow sticks, not, however, disguising the great flowing peppered beard of the man. "It's October 31st, St Erth's Day, and I was told the future of the Earth is what this club is about," he explained. His costume won the night's top prize.

The three Eaton brothers, John, Fredrik, and George, Toronto's leading department store merchants, were there dressed as the three musketeers, having rejected out of hand the suggestion that they dress as three Musketeers to reflect the fact that their stores were celebrating California week. The Mirvish family, down-market merchants famous for the huge "Honest Ed's" discount emporium, but equal purveyors of upscale art galleries and downtown theatres were there. Ed himself was done up as Sir John David Eaton and his wife, as Lady Eaton, and their son, David, the art collector, dressed and well made up as Paul Gaugin. Bank presidents were there, one indeed dressed as a pauper out of Charles Dickens or Victor Hugo. The most noticeable was the Reichmans, the biggest real estate developers in the world, who were dressed like the big new buildings they were doing at the World Financial Centre in New York ad were about to undertake t Londin's Canary Wharf. They received the night's award for the best collective costume ensemble. A still youthful Conrad Black, having made and lost and then maybe made again and then maybe lost again untold millions for himself if not shareholders, was there, dressed and behaving convincingly as his hero, Napoleon Bonaparte. And noticed by all, Dee Proulx, the ball's organizer, was dressed as the belle of the ball in a vast flowing organdy dress in shocking orange, masked in black and on her head, wearing an enormous, feathered play on a witch's black hat.

The event was already noisy and sensational as Simon, unmasked, stepped to the podium set up in front of the bandstand. He wore tails, a red-edged cape, and a top hat.

"Thank you, Rush, for brilliantly getting the ball into an appropriate mood of complex harmony. Let us see if our gamers here tonight can match that. I see you are all fabulously costumed and masked. I am dressed as I am sure you will recognize as Mandrake, the Magician, but at this moment, unmasked so that I may readily guide and assist you. Unless that is, someone else is wearing a Simon Kiss mask." That drew laughter.

"Anyway, I am here to give you "The Peace Game!"

That was followed by cheers.

"Actually, it has to be a sort of war and peace game. I have placed on each of the twenty tables here in the arcade four copies of the rules of the game. You have had in the last hour the time to make up your teams. Your players will face a five-power world with lots of incentives for war and only a few clever strategies for avoiding it. One may lead to a lasting peace. If you can get through to midnight and establish world peace, we will all get a bonus: The Government of Ontario will contribute $1 million to the Save the Children Fund."

This also brought loud applause.

"So, work and play hard at it and try not to be too disappointed if you all turn into warmongers - the playing of the game does not allow unrealistic peace idealism to dominate any side's gains, though it may have some influence. You must all try to play your sides realistically. Players, you have a final thirty minutes to get your teams to the tables and study the rules. Enjoy the game."

Simon was satisfied with the excitement not only in the arcade but throughout the club as he passed into his office, where Sabina, dressed as Swan Lake's dying swan, was waiting for him.

"I know it is you. Even in the white mask, you look beautiful, Sabina."

"As a kid, I always wanted to dance Swan Lake. My older sister said I was just right for the part."

"You never told me that. So, did you follow through with it?"

"For a time. When I was in mid-high school, I went to some pre-admission sessions at the National Ballet School. It turned out I wasn't least interested in giving my life to the mere chance of being an accomplished ballet dancer. It seemed, well, ballet training seemed a kind of a crap shoot at best, so I went to talk to Dee Proulx, who was the youngest teacher at my school at the time and already a kindred spirit. She was quite blunt: 'You are exactly right, Sabina: ballet is for those amazing *maigre* few who can move their bodies as if already caught within the balletomane's merciless prison. And, because they are so often pushed into it, they can't think of much else to do. You can. You don't need to narrow your chances so early in life. I'd drop it.' So, I did. But not without wanting to dance the dying swan in Swan Lake all my life."

Simon said, "Well, and here you are tonight, so beautifully costumed and poised as the swan. I cannot resist embracing you. Please allow me to dance with you later in the evening."

"Yes, later in the evening, Simon, my love."

He said, "Unfortunately, now I must chase you out. I must check on some outside things, and then I have to preside over the party gaming. See if you can find a good partner – I would avoid only Napoleon, who might try to conquer you and possibly those unwieldy Reichman buildings bumping into everyone."

She laughed and slipped out of his office. He called Tarasov.

"How are things?"

"Good. I just asked Cliff for a snack, and he's bringing me down some blinis - very thoughtful of you."

"No, he suggested that you have the best Russian food and vodka while I have a ball downtown."

"I am most appreciative of both of you. See you later tonight or tomorrow morning for our final exercises."

"Yes."

They rang off.

Back in the arcade, the gaming was going well. Simon had decided to use the methods of sociometry to depict how near or far the five powers were to each other through the course of the game. The five big red balls moved fluidly around the video screens as the various teams took each move.

At 10:00, the gaming and everything else was temporarily halted as David Bowie arrived and took to the bandstand. He announced what he called a new color phonic piece named and dedicated to 'the Peace Game.' He and a mix of his band and Rush played brilliantly for twelve minutes. It was followed by loud appreciation from the audience.

The gaming resumed. At 10:30, it looked like a group of three and a group of two world powers were gradually consolidating into two alliances from the groups playing at the twenty tables - the gist of the game was that alliances initially were brought together in war moves that still could achieve a genuine enduring peace. Simon had color-coded the results from each round of moves – the closer to full red, the closer the situation to war, then through purples until closer to a light pink, the closer to peace. The balls were all still red, as he had thought they would be at this point. But the players had so far managed to avoid any of the game-ending war defaults.

That held until 11:10, when something confused the players and horrified Simon. The screens were suddenly covered with fast-moving lines of code, which a few in the room recognized as machine language.

Simon knew that his Lakeview computer system was self-destroying and dumping the latest back game database to Worlds, and somehow that had overridden the computer system at the club managing the Halloween gaming.

People were already upset that their latest clever moves had been lost.

Simon went to the bandstand.

"Please, attention, everyone. Somehow our underlying machine processing has supplanted our game processing. I will try to correct this. I am very sorry - please expect a ten-minute interlude.

Simon headed over to the hub and, without even looking at the screens, began to rapidly key in the commands necessary to override the override, and within five minutes, the gaming screens were back to where they had been before the interruption, even with the latest moves by players He and everyone else was much relieved.

Simon went back to the bandstand and said, "I'm sorry about that. Please resume your gaming. I will ask the Ontario government to give us an additional ten minutes to make up for this error. I trust you will have until 12:10 to make your final moves."

Amid cheers of appreciation, Simon headed quickly to his office.

He placed a call to Lakeview. The normal phone line was dead. He wondered if the spooks were at work. He placed another call to his secret alternate line. That only showed a light. e. It was still alive. But no one answered.

Good, he thought at least that worked. That's how the emergency dump of back game files had been achieved, however messily at the receiving end at Worlds. But what the hell was going on at Lakeview that caused the worst-case scenario?

"Oh God, he thought: could it be that the backchannel was about to be exposed?

Part Five:
November 1983

Chapter 27

Walker was headed north in one of the first Apaches, the army's fastest new long-distance chopper.

His phone had rung earlier.

"What? Aw shit. Activate Plan C. Commence now with the Canadian military... Yes. Now! Now! I'll be there around midnight."

He had called Andrews. "Apache better be there. Can you take me up north to Ottawa?'

After a moment, he got the answer he wanted. All high pressure, light air. Get you there in maybe two and a half hours."

Get the Apache ready – I'll be there in 30 minutes.

He had called another number. "Warrington, maybe big trouble – I've activated. Plan C. You in surveillance detail?"

"Okay. Something seems to have gone wrong at the farmhouse. Take care of anything as necessary – I'll be up there by midnight latest."

He was rapidly preparing to leave his home, thinking through his contingency plan C when his phone rang again. It was his boss, General Roger Whittier, Chair of the Joint Chiefs of Staff.

"Goddam it, Walker, I told you to keep me informed. Deaver just called me to say that something weird is happening, maybe exposing whatever you're up to in Toronto. It better not get to the President - he is a purist. He wants no contact with the enemy. He wants nothing that gives them comfort. He thinks we can defeat the Soviets with strong American will and without any backchannel assistance. If this is that back channel I recently heard about, can you give me any reason not to have you carted off to Leavenworth?"

"Look: you want me to deal with this, or just take me down?

"You better explain, quick."

"Let me deal with it first. Then I'll explain. I've got it covered. Stand by."

He rang off.

As he left his house, the phone rang again. He realized Deaver at the CIA had just upped the ante.

Chapter 28

Thinking back on it, Russ Russell could see why everything had happened at once. His involvement had been mainly his own initiative. After the work Sabina Hurst had hired him to do in Philadelphia, he obtained new information about the danger to Simon Kiss' life. This was because Sabina had asked him to keep an eye on Simon around Toronto."

Russell, a loyal friend of the Hurst family, took the challenge very seriously. He followed Simon's movements enough through October to realize that something was up at Lakeview Farm. He discovered that Lakeview was under surveillance by other parties. He knew Simon had a big computer installation there.

Now, he was approaching Lakeview very stealthily from a half mile away to avoid being caught up in the surveillance perimeter. He had managed to do that twice so far. This was the third time. A night he knew Simon had to be in Toronto.

He had ensconced himself on October 31st at an adjacent farm to the east that was apparently vacant and just sold. He hid out in a deteriorated outbuilding that had nearly collapsed to the ground. It gave him a good view of Lakeview. He had decided to stay there all night. He was getting off to a snooze when he heard sounds from the farm he was beside. A van had arrived. From the sign on their van, it looked like a small film crew was occupying the old abandoned farmhouse itself.

Russ soon realized that the film crew was being guarded by a mean-looking big guy with an automatic gun sometimes in view. Russ thought he should get closer. Crawling along an old stone wall, he got himself close enough to hear the talk of the three men. Most of it was in Russian. He wondered whether it was a "Soviet stake-out or a KGB stake-out."

Russell withdrew to the rotting ruin along the western line of the property. He calibrated the situation. He figured Simon would be back from the Halloween Ball at Worlds very late that night. Russ had been told by Sabina that Simon's electronic strategy games in the club's arcade would be featured at the widely publicized event. So why was there any interest in Lakeview?

He wondered if one or more of the surveillance parties, and especially this 'film crew', might also use this opening with Simon gone to do something at Lakeview. He decided he should use the cover of night to slip into Lakeview himself and check what was happening there. He didn't want Simon to be compromised by any such raids if he could do anything about it.

At 10:30, Russ moved out of his hide-out and crept in stages across the field. It was still a working hay field, and he moved between hay bales on the field. Unless someone had infrared capability sweeping the field, he could go unseen and under surveillance beams, which he had himself once installed at the farmhouse complex.

Sabina had given Russ a good description of the layout of the house. She had told Russ that Simon's main computer setup was in a big room in the basement. She gave him other details he had memorized about the interior and exterior of Lakefield, even the nearby barns, which she had walked him through one morning when Simon was busy. She said the whole property and the main farmhouse were alarmed "to the teeth." Russ had eluded the first alarm perimeter by slipping under a frost-heaved lowest rail along its eastern fence line. He had avoided the motion sensors. As he proceeded from hay bale to hay bale, he thought that his movement might trigger searchlights and alarm sirens over the whole area at any moment.

He made it to the gardens surrounding the main house. Although he was now beside the house, possibly even more vulnerable to various sensors, the gardens afforded greater visual cover. He still moved very slowly.

He rethought his commitment to Sabina. It was information on the status of the situation she wanted, not intervention. But how could he get information without somehow getting into the main house?

A plan formed in his mind: why not suddenly appear at the already well-lit front, walk to the front door, and then simply knock on it? Chances were that just walking up the front walk would only trigger some warning inside the house, as opposed to all the perimeter alarms. The various third parties watching would be delayed, just wondering who he was, while in the meantime, he just might be admitted by Simon's housekeepers. If one or more of the third parties did come in, he would simply say he was private security. Even that way, he might pick up useful information. The more he considered it, the better he liked his chances.

He didn't want to move very far along the front walk before he might trip some alarm for being off the walk, so he moved slowly another few feet and then simply popped up and strode to the front door. He knocked and pressed the doorbell. No alarms. After a minute or two, Mrs. Forbes opened the door, and he reminded her that they had met once or twice, and he was the Hurst's private security guy. Did she mind if he came in?

"What did you say your name was?"

"Russ Russell. Here is my card."

"Okay, yes, I've seen you here. So, Mr. Russell, please do come in. At this moment, I am almost alone in the house – my husband Cliff has disappeared somewhere. He served the gentleman downstairs supper over an hour back. I can't imagine them talking this long."

"You are very kind to admit me. Perhaps I can help. My duty is to look after Dr. Kiss' interests."

"Well, yes, this is Dr. Kiss' farm. It has been in his family for quite a while, but he's not here now. How could you help?"

"Perhaps, allow me to slip downstairs and see what's up down there?"

"Well, Dr. Tarasov is down there, in the computer room. But, yes, that would be good. I rarely go down there. There are all kinds of electrical equipment in the big room. I have no idea what goes on down there, but it must be important. Dr. Kiss is often down there, and now his friend, Dr. Tarasov, has been here, off and on, all the last week."

Hilda showed Russell to the main stairs to the basement.

Russell slipped down the stairs, turned right as she had directed him to, and stopped. He could hear a conversation. After listening for a few moments, he could not believe what he was hearing.

Two persons arguing the wisdom of one of the guys wanting not only to steal whatever Simon Kiss and presumably the other guy in there were doing together through a Soviet-American back channel but doing so to use it in a way that the other guy, sounding like Simon's friend Tarasov seemed to approve of and saying he thought Simon would approve of. Russ found this bewildering and most unsettling.

At first, he thought it was better to break into the conversation, but he withdrew. He opened a door into a dark room down the hall to consider his options. The light coming through the door as he opened it illuminated the figure of a man on the floor lying against the far wall. Russ closed the door noiselessly, turned on his penlight, and shone it around the room. There were boxes, electronic stuff, and some old floor lamps.

Along one wall, his flashlight beam shone onto a figure sitting up against the wall. The man was motionless. He concluded the man might well be Cliff Forbes. He went over and felt for a pulse but found none. The man was dead. Russ had to rethink his options.

He was doing so when alarms began to sound all over the house. Russ could see through the basement windows that many outside floodlights had turned on. It was too late for an escape option. His best option now was to withdraw behind the boxes and await developments. He could already hear approaching vehicles skidding to a halt and adding to the din of the house alarm system.

Someone rushed by in the basement hall. He heard a Russian-accented voice shouting, "Get the hell out of here while you can, Sommerfeld!" He heard what sounded like a door slamming further down the hall. He recalled the floorplan – it was an emergency door to the outside gardens.

Upstairs and outside the house, pandemonium reigned.

The first surveillance team receiving information of apparent mysterious developments underway within the house that had caused the computer dump from there to Worlds Club was the police group – Toronto police, receiving the message in the same surveillance vehicle with the Mounties and the FBI agents. It was from the Toronto Police Chief of Detectives, Colin Miservy. He commented to the Police Chief beside him, "Sir, that was an emergency procedure from Dr. Kiss' farm in Lakeview. We better find out what's going on out there and try to be the first to do so!"

Miservy called the police forces surveillance unit and told them that something had gone wrong at Lakeview and that the secret Soviet-American war gaming had likely been compromised at Lakeview and to go in. The team had waited to see if the other teams had made a move. When nothing happened, they decided they better follow orders. The joint police unit roared into the driveway at Lakeview.

Seeing the joint police FBI group screeching into Lakeview, the combined CIA-Canadian intelligence group quickly followed the police car. The joint American-Canadian military intelligence team then roared in.

To the east, just before the general alarms and spotlights went on, the three-man KGB team Russell had seen at the adjacent farm had for a while been moving on their stomachs into the eastern gardens near the house, where they hunkered down to consider their own next move as suddenly various dark vans and vehicles poured onto the Lakeview Farms main driveways.

Sommerfeld, heading away from the farmhouse, saw three men with heavy automatic guns headed toward him. He had no idea who they were, but he ducked into a protective sunflower garden.

At the same time, a hay wagon followed by a dark SUV without its lights on slowly headed down the long twisty lane in the farmland to the south with only a single flashlight guiding it. It was within 200 yards of the main house at Lakeview. Two men got out. One grabbed a mortar weapon from the hay. The other set up a camera. Sommerfeld had not joined them as planned, but even so, their own covert mission was underway. The mortar shells were to be aimed well away from the house, and then the explosions lighting up the house could be captured on videotape. The expected explosions, with their supplied media commentary, leaked to global media, would ensure world opinion would be riveted to what had happened near Toronto on Halloween night. A plot that the crouching Sommerfeld, having just escaped from the Lakeview basement, knew all about and now wished he had never agreed to, let alone ever belonged to the group at all.

As to the mayhem at the farmhouse itself, there were enough law enforcement and intelligence units coming into Lakeview to surround the house and then enter it and secure the interior.

The FBI police unit dispatched a team of three to go down to secure the basement. There, they found Tarasov and Russell politely waiting for them.

Mrs. Forbes upstairs had kept shouting, "Please find Cliff down there. He's my husband!"

Ivan said quietly, "I am afraid her husband Cliff is dead – his body is down the hall in the next room."

At ground level, the Can-Am joint intelligence team, headed by CIA Deputy Director, Bill Warrington, entered the farmhouse. He flashed his identity card at the Canadian and FBI police group on the main floor.

"You're short - where's the rest of your police team?"

The police team said nothing.

Warrington yelled, "Look, we need everybody together to work this out, or we will all look ridiculous. CIA has the lead over FBI here."

The FBI lead said, "We need to secure the damn place first. Some of our police personnel are downstairs; some are upstairs. Obviously, we need a sit-down. We can use the big dining room in there to work this out." He looked at Hilda. "Missus, we are also looking everywhere for your husband. In the meantime, would it be possible for you to please get us some coffee?"

She used to and appreciated polite orders, saying, "Of course, gentlemen, I will start our largest coffee machine." As she headed to the kitchens, she thought maybe busy work would take some of her minds off the disappearance of her husband.

Downstairs, Ivan said to the police, "You will find the system here of no interest in its present state - it has self-destructed its own hard drive, thanks to all this outside interference. It no longer has any files whatsoever." Ivan was also thinking, where did Russell disappear to"

The police brought Ivan upstairs, only to find the scene changed there. Some guys still had their guns out.

Warrington immediately spotted Ivan. "That guy could be a Soviet agent. Frisk him and give him special care."

The last group going into Lakeview was the military intelligence group. The joint Canadian-American armed forces intelligence team surveilling Lakeview had held off when they realized the other groups were suddenly going in - after all, they had three army trucks full of crack Canadian troops two concessions over ready to back them up. Plus, they held all the real information about what was going on at Lakeview.

The heavy thrumming of an approaching helicopter became almost deafening as it landed a few more soldiers on the front driveway. They increased the crowd in the house.

Warrington said to the crowd around him in the front hall, "Everyone: we are all friendly security services dedicated to, well, Canadian peace and good order." He had garbled the last part of Canada's famous Constitutional commitment to "peace, order, and good government," but the Canadians present were nonetheless appreciative.

"The principals can meet in the dining room - it has a sizable table. We will be served coffee. That's all I can guarantee."

They were all getting comfortable when the thrumming sound of another helicopter was heard. It landed next to the Lakeview driveway.

General Walker strode out of the chopper and pushed his way through the crowd of soldiers there now.

Warrington said, "General Walker, glad you could make it here. You wouldn't be pulling rank again, would you?"

"You got that right. This site is now officially a joint Can-Am military intelligence exercise over which Brigadier General White here from Canadian military intelligence and I are the senior commanders." He was literally pulling General White into the dining room,

"You can't just override other security services like that."

"Oh yeah? Consider these points, then. Number one, we alone, unlike all of you people, know exactly what is or was happening here, and that is in the national interest of both countries.

"Number two, the horse is out of the barn – none of the activity of interest is left here; it is a heavily computerized operation that was disturbed and has now gone down, dead. Number three, if we aren't all on the script, at some point, a parade of the press will arrive and not buy the cover story. For example, I told you not to have any flashing vehicle lights, and I arrive to more lights than a fucking carnival out there. Geez. I don't know yet what actually happened here, but we joint military have and are prepared to direct and share with you the only workable cover story for what's going on that involves so many units. That story must be that this is just a secured joint services exercise, with many different agencies involved, including surrounding the place with armored troop carriers."

Only Warrington protested, "For Christ's sake, Walker, it's now not just you and I that know what really was going on here."

"All the more reason for you to bug out of it - it's not our fault everyone else's presence here could ruin the international joint military exercise side of this. And who is this guy you have in that pretty steel bracelet?"

Then he took a closer look at Ivan.

"Well, well, lookee whom we got here: Comrade Tarasov," said Walker. He knew Tarasov indirectly from numerous photographs of him at computer social simulation conferences that Simon Kiss had attended. He had long known Tarasov was on the Soviet side of Simon Kiss' back channel.

Ivan said, "I managed to get a photo of the guy who interrupted me and who may well have caused all this. He managed to get away after he tied me up in the computer room. You may recognize him," Ivan said to Walker.

Walker at once recognized Sommerfeld from Mathematics Trust days. "I sure as hell recognize him. That is one David Sommerfeld, much wanted by the FBI and erstwhile Acting Director of the Mathematics Trust. Went to school with Simon Kiss, didn't he?"

It was a rhetorical question.

And it was at that point that Toronto Chief of Detectives Colin Miservy arrived on the scene. He had heard this last statement by Walker.

Miservy quickly introduced himself and said, "The FBI explained enough to indicate some kind of war gaming was being shared between the Americans and the Soviets through a back channel set up here in the Toronto area. The police only went in when the computer here downloaded everything to the computer at Worlds club in the city, which we knew could only be because some kind of emergency was occurring at Lakeview. We all now suspect this is all related to the use of Simon Kiss for secret backchannel American-Soviet war games."

Everyone turned to him. Miservy continued, "But we also know that one of the people who were here - one David Sommerfeld, recently thought to reside in the Toronto area - is a person of interest in the murders of the Honorable Michael Keefe and Martin Davies and that he is a left-wing guy on the FBI wanted to list down in the States and recently by the Philadelphia police in connection with a death in that city."

There were some looks of astonishment around the room - everyone knew from Ivan that Sommerfeld had just been on the scene at Lakeview. Walker provided Miservy with that information.

"Well then, he clearly is the person of main interest in all this. But we seem to have a convergence of otherwise sometimes conflicting agency interests, which will indeed require sorting out before any of us can leave," concluded Miservy.

Walker replied, "You've got that right - we all need a cover for what happened here. Joint military intelligence is providing that."

At that moment, an officer appeared at the top of the basement stairs.

"Sir," he said, looking at Miservy; we will be bringing up the body of the houseman. Will someone break the news to his wife?"

Warrington said, "I will do that – I talked to her earlier." He went off to do the grim duty.

When Miservy was filled in, he said, "We'll need an experienced crime scene team here – it would normally be Durham Regional police – they might prefer the OPP in this situation, though."

Walker nodded to Miservy, who said, "Go ahead - General White will get them a pass-through. Strict confidentiality, of course." Miservy went to arrange it.

At that moment, they all heard Mrs. Forbes' loud weeping from the kitchen. Warrington returned from the kitchen. "I've left someone with her. She mentioned her husband had a bad heart she knew would just give out at some point. I didn't mention any other possible cause of what may have happened to him. Let that shock come later."

Ivan spoke to this. "Sommerfeld told me before he escaped that he had temporarily subdued the man. Even if it was some temporary disablement, it could quite likely have triggered the heart attack or whatever."

Ivan was put under close guard in the living room, and a dozen of the leading military, police, and intelligence people went into the dining room for their sit-down. They began to work on Walker's proposed modus vivendi under the cover of a "joint military operation.

An hour earlier, outside the farmhouse, Major Gallipoliov held an arm just inside the fence between the house's eastern gardens and the adjacent field. He was followed by two others from his special KGB team who intended to disrupt and destroy the back game inside the farmhouse. He waved, and they went over the fence. Since the perimeter alarm had just gone off, they were no longer concerned about tripping them. The three men crouched in the gardens about 50 to 100 yards east of the main house, now completely lit and had a good view of the unexpected activity within, just beyond the sunflowers nodding at them in the garden closest to the house. The three men had enough firepower to take out anyone in the house, especially Tarasov, their prime target, and then disappear back to the next farm and escape from there.

Before they could do that, the first of several vehicles started to arrive at the farmhouse. Gallipoli had to think things through and motioned his partners to conceal themselves in the outer hedges and hunker down for a while. The while took the next hour as the farmhouse steadily filled with officialdom, and helicopters buzzed the property.

Gallipoli was the only one of them who had war experience. He was so thoroughly briefed on most of what was now going down at Lakeview that he was truly amazed when he heard distant mortar fire and then sensed the incoming shells. He was not able to warn his advancing colleagues. In a few moments, they were all three blown to pieces.

Closer to the house, Sommerfeld was already down on the ground in a sunflower garden when much of the back gardens went up in the three explosions. They covered him in the dirt.

Inside the house, the explosions sent everyone in the dining room to the floor. One of the house's big windows and some of the observatory windows were shattered. Loud expletives were uttered by the men now staring at each other under the dining-room table.

Outside, three KGB bodies lay amongst destroyed gardens. Nearer the house, Sommerfeld, in the sunflower bed, was stunned for a moment but otherwise had survived the shelling. He managed to get on his feet and limped away from the house as fast as he could when he was grabbed by a Mountie, not too confused to see and do his duty.

Inside the house, the people on the dining room floor smelled the acrid smoke of the exploding mortar rounds. Moments later, they began to hear the thump-thump-thump of yet another approaching helicopter.

"It better not be the President," said an American wag among them.

"As long as it's not the Prime Minister," said a Canadian wag.

Walker said, "Would you guys shut up? Who could have a new chopper coming in here?"

"Probably the Durham Region Police with the crime scene crew," said Miservy. "It couldn't be the press already."

"Anyway," General White said, "Those sounded like mortar rounds – where the hell did they come from? Walker, you got any idea?"

"Nothing surprises me anymore about this situation. Let's make sure our guys find out!"

Chapter 29

The now even more military arriving by trucks quickly secured the farms to the south and east of Lakeview, even as the Durham Region police chopper had flown off. The police within it were upset they had not decided to follow a fast-moving black Chevy suburban a few miles south of the scene – it had even been passed on the concession road by military trucks coming into Lakeview. Now it was gone.

Within five minutes, a Canadian army captain came in and gave what he thought was the grim news, "Looks like the mortar fire came from the farm south-west of the house, landed approximately 50 yards east of the house, and unfortunately, there are three dead guys out there, along the hedges, sir!"

Walker said, "Shit. Our guys?"

"No identification found yet. So, I don't know who they are for sure, but here's a hint - one guy had a Russian-English phrase book."

"Okay," said Miservy. "General Walker, we can offer the services of the Forensic Centre in Toronto for processing and identification of the bodies. They do good work."

"No," said Walker. "This now has far too much international sensitivity. General White, could you arrange for them to be taken to a secure military base with forensic processing facilities and a morgue? They can bring in any additional expertise as necessary?"

"Yes, that makes good sense, General Walker. It would be a circus in downtown Toronto, especially when the media get onto it."

Walker said, okay, let's start from the beginning and start questioning Tarasov."

They were about to do so when two more astonishing things happened.

First, a filthy Sommerfeld was escorted into the house.

Walker was delighted. "So, now we have Sommerfeld, as Tarasov told us, still on the scene. Lucky to be alive. Sit him down in the living room, not too close to Tarasov."

But secondly, even as that was occurring, a man emerged from the basement, to everyone's surprise, walked into the dining room, and said, "I think I might help you with some of these things."

Russell joined everyone who sat back down at the crowded dinner table.

General Walker knew most of what was going on but could not account for the mortar shelling and knew he was missing some other things; he welcomed the newcomer, "And what god dammed service do you represent - the Parks Service?"

"My own – I'm a private detective. Russ Russell. My card?" He handed Walker his card. "Actually, I can vouch for him," said Miservy.

Russell continued, "I'm on this scene because I keep a routine eye on Lakeview every few days for the owner. I was remaining in the basement behind the furnace, awaiting an appropriate time to come upstairs."

"The owner being Simon Kiss?" said Miservy.

"Yes. The family."

Warrington from the CIA was going to take over the questioning, but Walker, impressed with Miservy, winked at Warrington to hold off as if to say, "Let the locals do it for a while."

Though it was true Simon Kiss had asked him to check things out at Lakeview from time to time, Russell was not going to explain he had been retained by Sabina Hurst to keep Simon out of trouble. Simon would never forgive him if he brought Sabina into all this."

"So, when did you get here today, and what have you done or seen since you got here?" asked Miservy.

"Okay, let me take your questions in that order. I was in the area at the farm to the east since mid-day Halloween Eve. I decided to stay overnight in an outbuilding on the farm to the east because I became aware of a variety of surveillance teams in vehicles on the roads in the vicinity. That made me uneasy. Then, during the early evening, a group of three men arrived at the same farm. It is a property that is vacant and was recently sold."

"So," said Walker.

"I got closer to observing these people. There was a bright moon. They were carrying golf bags into the house. Two of them had what appeared to be large binoculars, the kind I recognized were adapted for night use. Most interestingly, Russian was being spoken, and one man was openly brandishing a Russian-made Makarov semi-automatic pistol. I concluded this could well be a Soviet KGB operation since I know that Dr. Kiss is active in the development of some sensitive military computer work."

"What do you know about that?"

"Oh, nothing much at all. But it sure made me wonder about who my companions were on the vacant farm. Anyway, I retreated around 8:00 p.m. and observed both farmhouses. I saw Dr. Kiss leave at 3:00. I knew he was headed for his club in Toronto because there was a big Halloween ball at his club that night which was featuring his electronic games.

"Quite a cut-up, isn't he," chuckled Walker.

"I noticed lights were on in the basement computer room, which I concluded meant Dr. Tarasov, with whom Simon sometimes worked, was there. I decided I would slip across the field and somehow get into the main house to deal with a possible KGB attack on Tarasov. Then I noticed someone entering the house through a basement window.

"I wondered who else might have seen that, especially my close neighbors in the vacant farmhouse. I waited fifteen minutes. There was no movement beside me, so I started to scramble through the field below Lakeview's own scanning motion sensors, which, as it happened, I had installed. I waited in the outside gardens for another half hour. I had to decide how to get into the house. I couldn't figure out a way to get past the door and window alarms."

"Which you yourself had installed," said Miservy.

"Yeah. The only solution I could come up with was to crawl around to the front walk, just before the front door, and then all of a sudden appear in a way that might not trigger the alarms if they had not been set for the front walkway and door. I knew that option was in the alarm system."

"Which you yourself had installed," said Walker.

"Yeah, okay, okay. Anyway, it worked. I figured I was spotted by at least some of the surveillance units, but I would have some time inside because they would be going through a decision process as to whether my solitary appearance should trigger going from surveillance mode to going in, given the possible inter-service complications."

"Smart guy," said Walker.

"Well, I've been around. Anyway, I presented myself to the house lady, Mrs. Forbes, and the next thing I knew, she was asking me to look for her husband, who had disappeared downstairs, serving "Dr. Tarasov" his dinner back at 7:30. So, I offered to go down and investigate. She agreed, and I did."

"Then what?"

"Well, you might ask. When I got to the bottom of the stairs and hallway and headed to the computer room to the right, I could hear voices in an intense conversation. I didn't know who they were, but it sounded like two people were discussing the merits of the use of a strategy game, whatever that was, to develop more important global policy lessons for the world than just Soviet-American military war gaming. One guy actually said that dramatizing the project at Lakeview would help get media coverage for the wider cause."

Miservy said, "Did they agree?"

"I can't say for sure. Anyway, that was all I could make out before I heard the men fussing and the alarm systems started going off, and I guess you guys started pouring into the house. So, I quickly headed the other way down the hall and into a big dark basement room at the other end of the computer room. I held the door open for a moment. The light it let in shone on someone lying against the far wall. I shut the door, turned on my penlight, went over, and determined that the man was likely the house man, Mr. Forbes, and that he was quite dead."

"Yes, we have since found him there."

"As the noise increased upstairs and I heard people coming downstairs, I ducked into the furnace room and his behind the furnace to figure out what I should do next. I was still there when the explosions occurred. After that, I basically hid until things quieted down a bit, and I heard an approaching helicopter. I figured whatever was big had already happened and was over. And I came upstairs to offer my assistance. I hope that helps."

General Walker took over.

"Yes, it does indeed. We now know more about the three dead bodies in the east gardens, and I think we know someone to ask about the mortar fire that landed near us in this house. Whoever – and it sure looks like Sommerfeld - got in to get a chance to talk to Tarasov, he must have killed Mr. Forbes to do so. The matters they were discussing implicate them both in messing with a top-secret military activity designed to preserve and avoid destabilizing our precarious nuclear balance. Maybe the mortar fire was designed to expose that little exercise. We're monitoring news outlets."

Walker looked around at everyone.

"So, now it's time to talk to the guys in the living room, who were the two people you probably overheard in the basement. Miservy, could you bring one in for a chat? I guess that's all we need from you at this point, Russell – you can take a seat in the living room, too, please. No conversation, though. Have a cup of coffee."

"Sure," said Russell. Russell passed Tarasov being brought into the dining room.

He got a surprise as he entered the living room. There, Sommerfeld was still seated. Russell saw that he was the man who had been staring out the window at the Mathematics Trust offices on the day of the possible homicide.

In the dining room, Walker looked at Ivan and said, "You and that Sommerfeld has got some 'splaining' to do. We thought we'd begin with you, Comrade Tarasov."

Tarasov managed a smile. "I'm not sure what "splaining" means. Is that like a sprained ankle?"

"You're going to get more than that if you don't start telling us what was going on down there between you and Sommerfeld."

"Okay, fair enough. I gather it's your lead here right now, or at least as long as the Canadians here yield it to you. I don't need to explain to you what Simon Kiss and I have been doing here in the past few weeks. I'll let you explain that as you wish."

"Or not," said Walker.

"Exactly. Anyway, Sommerfeld surprised me in the computer room downstairs – he knocked me away from the computer keyboard so I couldn't ditch the game or raise the alarm. I let him try to talk me into a whole different project using Rondo to work on global solutions to non-military problems. I have to say he, Sommerfeld is quite a piece of work – he almost talked me into it and out of my pretense with him."

"The private detective down there heard you - he said it sounded like you agreed."

"Well, I agreed only to his general premise that sharing human social simulations across the world on non-military uses and other global policy issues is a good idea. And I only did that to give myself time to free myself from being tied up. When I had tied him up, I told him, 'If you have such ideas, this is not the way to further them.' Then when I heard the alarms, I foolishly let him vamoose. I didn't want to be seen with him. That was a mistake."

"Okay," said Walker. "It seems Sommerfeld is working outside of, if not against, any governmental authority. Let's call him in. Tarasov, you can wait this out in the living room, and we'll call you in again later."

After Tarasov was taken out, Sommerfeld was brought in.

The man was looking utterly defeated.

Walker let Miservy begin the questioning. "So, Sommerfeld, Tarasov has given us a clear description of what you two were considering down in the computer room. What's your version?"

"I don't deny I tried to talk him into sharing the Rondo software for better human uses. He seemed interested."

"Was that before or after he escaped your bonds, and then you were, in turn, tied up?"

Sommerfeld had decided not to play prisoners' dilemma with Tarasov. He trusted Tarasov's version of what Simon was doing to evolve Rondo slowly and steadily to more civilian uses. He had long since realized the real foe was the unknown group he reported to, supposedly wanting to speed up "progressive social science." The group who was behind the MFD murders. The supposedly progressive but anonymous group he had foolishly worked for. He was about to see if Tarasov would agree to let Sommerfeld go so he could learn more precisely what that group was. He had to continue his whole confession to help Tarasov out of his jam.

"Yes, we struggled, but he won and tied me up. I had first hoped he would give me what was necessary to build a copy of Rondo for more progressive global policy uses. We were discussing that general idea and why he thought Simon's patient way was still the best one, and I was about to confess that I was now, in a sense, a double agent, about to act against the group I reported to, when we heard all the noise upstairs, and he untied me and let me run down the basement hall to an emergency door leading outside to the gardens."

Miservy said, "There's a dead man down there - the houseman, Cliff Forbes. What do you know about him?"

Sommerfeld looked down at his hands. When he raised his head, there were tears in his eyes.

"I just now heard that he is dead, and I freely confess that I am guilty of that. I am prepared to face the consequences of the law on that. I am miserable about it. It is not enough that I decided to turn on the group I was reporting to and that I now think governments will come to value what Tarasov and Kiss are trying to do and come to accept a broader vision for it. That poor man died at my hands, though I had no intent to kill him. I was given training that assured me the method I used on him was simply a temporary disablement – the victim was supposed to have regained consciousness within twenty minutes."

"Who gave you that instruction?"

"Someone here in Toronto assigned to me by the group and who was one the other two guys on the team that fired the mortar rounds – again with no intent to kill anyone. I can describe him for you." He did.

A senior Mountie said, "That describes someone we already have a file on."

"So, you want us to believe you have turned on your group, huh?"

"I have not trusted them since realizing that the first Ontario Government death was murder, intended or otherwise. And then another one – my friend, Martin!"

"You must have had a connection with those?" said Miservy.

"Well, again, I did not realize whomever I reported to would take such horrific actions simply to cover up the theft of a copy of the Rondo tape."

"And yet you shared their 'vision,'" said Miservy.

"Well, to begin with, the broader vision for Rondo is something I now realize both Simon and Ivan Tarasov also fully share with me, but they obviously do not think the time is yet quite right for broader use of Rondo. As to my mysterious superiors in this, when it comes to it, you will find out only one possible lead from me about who I have been working for. I was gullible and stupid. To get their assistance to restore my own reputation and Davies' career, I guess I subconsciously let their identity remain unknown to me, as was their strict instruction. They simply provided me with the ultimate progressive seeming peace objective and the resources to pursue that. I mean, I never suspected lives would be lost and people killed for the progressive work I thought I was involved in."

Miservy said, "Well, presumably, you can provide us with any possible leads to that group you have?"

"Yes. One time I called a number, and it got right through to the top of the group. He was obviously upset about that. It is probably on my phone records. It was a Houston area code."

Sommerfeld went back to holding his head in disgrace and regret. He slowly looked up, " I am very sorry to say that I can provide no other information. I was just an idealistic fool and their willing tool up here. I assumed they were just decent, idealistic wealthy people who would themselves be easily compromised and their lives and careers compromised if their progressive tendencies were found out."

Walker snorted, "What kind of 'decent people' could murder other people?"

"As I concluded, no decent people, of course. It is clear to me now that they have some dark purpose. I know nothing of their true objectives, but obviously, they are convinced whatever it is – and I now suspect right-wing uses of Simon's system – the end justifies any means."

Walker seemed bemused.

"Why did you think 'the time is right' for the progressive non-military uses of Simon's stuff, yet Kiss and Tarasov do not?"

"Again, the idea was Simon's platform should be open for gaming many issues in the global situation, not just strategic war scenarios of interest to the military. And, if you are transforming things, the time is never right, is it? A transformation is not a change that meets gentle resistance. I guess that I am more impatient than Simon. I thought the time was way overdue, not just 'right.' But the odd thing is, Simon, would call me from time to time and ask me what I was doing to find a context for broader use of Rondo."

"What," said Walker. This was new.

"I could never figure him out. He actually called me in the district once and told me he had left his briefcase at a booth in a restaurant there and wondered if I might pick it up for him. It seemed like a crazy thing, and I decided not to do it. I thought it might be a setup. Simon seemed to behave like an automaton in each of those calls. I still wonder what triggered him to call that way. I passed on some of the stuff he told me to the group I reported to. I maybe should have suggested instead that Simon see a psychiatrist, as I now recall those calls. The last one in August was from the airport in Montreal – he kept encouraging me to do progressive things. Anyway, none of that spares me of my stupid association with those who deliberately killed other men, including Martin Davies, a good and equally duped friend, and then just now, my own accidental but negligent killing of the houseman."

Miservy said, "Yeah - go tell that to the dead man's wife. But before that, what can you tell us about the deadly sound and light show that just occurred outside?"

"It was partly my idea. The group wanted some serious attention-getting that would discredit Kiss and his military uses of Rondo. I arranged for the mortar attack that was deliberately aimed away from the house itself."

Walker muttered, "Three more deaths at your hands. That makes seven."

Sommerfeld groaned.

Tarasov was again being brought in from the living room and was given a summary of what Sommerfeld had said.

"He and that group, whoever they are sure, jumped to conclusions – we haven't successfully gamed even military scenarios to our satisfaction yet. They're still in the research and test stage. We've only helped preserve a precarious nuclear stand-off. Doing a bunch of global policy games would also fall far short of the drama and saliency of doing war-gaming. It's surprising how few people care enough for mere human advancement in the world or build a better model of the world within some "limits to growth" constraint."

Walker clarified, "You mean the Meadows' book, the Italian one with gloomy conclusions about the Earth's fate from a computer simulation of continued exponential global growth with only finite resources?"

"Yes. That was ten years ago. Since then, the Meadows have been disappointed. It was news for a while, and they were thinking the world would stop and take notice. They, too, wanted to run before we can even crawl with global policy processes."

A Canadian colonel entered the room and stated, somewhat breathlessly, "Sirs, the bodies of the three men killed along the outer hedges by the mortar shelling have been evacuated as General White directed."

"Thanks," said Walker. "Where's General White?"

"He went with them because of ultra-priority. He said he'd be back tomorrow.

"Okay, thanks."

Walker turned back to Sommerfeld.

"Whatever and whomever your group, they will now likely join the chorus they started that Simon and his military friends be shut down."

Sommerfeld looked bitterly back at Walker. "That's the problem, isn't it? Because you are so richly resourced, your military and intelligence guys think they can do anything important ahead of the rest of us that you can advance the science of strategy faster than any broader human endeavor could. Because the modern military leads the way – the strategy of wars and avoidance of wars leads even the best of you to think you are the facilitators of important human change. Well, there's far more to global strategy than just war or its avoidance, and to me, you are badly mistaken in that."

Walker said, "Okay, you've had your rant, Sommerfeld. You can now get out of our sight. Take him away, Miservy - you can start with charges in Mr. Forbes' death and whatever you can hang on him criminally about the government murders. Philadelphia, for that matter. You will have to keep it quiet and keep us in intelligence posted. Nothing at all, ever, about the KGB deaths here. Frankly, I think I can rely on you better than anyone to get to the bottom of Sommerfeld's involvement. And no statements to the press without our approval - you must go through General White and me."

Miservy said, "That won't work here unless you have got both Canadian and American higher-level clearance to hush everything up under your cover of a joint army intelligence "exercise." Do you have that clearance, General Walker? General White isn't here now."

"If we don't have that now, we will have."

Warrington said, "I do think we have reason to ask Simon Kiss some pointed questions about what he knew about any of this."

Sommerfeld spoke once more, "I think you will get very little from him about his contacts with me for the simple reason I doubt Simon realizes much or anything about his own sometimes strange mental state. He seems, well, as I told you, he seemed strangely distracted whenever he has contacted me over the years since university."

Walker said, "Okay until we talk to Kiss, that's enough from you. In the meantime, we maintain the noisy joint military exercise cover here. If the media want explosions, we better get another set of explosions underway – a very big joint exercise happening here!"

Chapter 30

By 2:00 a.m., the morning after Halloween, Simon had saved the downloaded back game results and its latest database on a separate hard drive in the basement of Worlds.

Though exhausted and not knowing the situation at Lakeview and the possibly dire consequences for him, he could not resist opening the data Tarasov had entered from the latest runs in Moscow and Washington to his office computer.

He graphed the results from the latest war game runs from both sides and immediately confirmed his prediction of very uncertain consequences for the purposes of a continuing nuclear balance. Rapaport's adjustments to the programming had mainly allowed him to be more precise about the uncertainty produced by bi-modal behavior tendencies within each side's leadership. Their model now reflected current bi-modal realities, and alas, the greater the uncertainty, the greater the risks of nuclear destabilization. He fell asleep, wondering how he would deliver this dark result to Walker.

He came awake at 6:00 a.m., November 1st, refreshed from a deep three-hour sleep, and immediately wrote his report to Walker. The best he could come up with was that perhaps Reagan's election had, in essence, produced a whole new interval for the nuclear balance game, requiring a new series of moves to see if the necessary cooperative stabilization pattern would re-emerge.

Simon realized he had committed his own most fundamental error. Not structuring strategy sequences in terms of their interval phasing: 1983, with Reagan's election, had commenced a new interval, not continued the previous interval. The 1983 results could only serve as a baseline for a new interval of moves, an interval that would continue through at least to the end of Reagan's term unless disrupted by new critical changes in the behavioral tendencies of the Kremlin power structure. He cursed himself as he thought of all that had happened when the only value of what he was doing with Tarasov amounted to defining a baseline of initial moves for the next interval until either or both sides made another "move."

Simon went to his car phone. It would not identify Worlds as the source of his subsequent calls. He called Sabina first.

"Sabina, it's me. I'm calling from my car.

"Simon, dearest, unless I miss my guess, you are in serious trouble. Do you know Lakeview has been raided? Big explosions. Mind you, the story for the media has been put out that it is only a joint American-Canadian military intelligence training 'exercise,' not anything 'real'"

"Well, I assumed something explosive had happened – that was what the dumping of my military strategy work on Rondo over to Worlds last night was all about. Sorry, it interrupted the Halloween gaming."

"Simon, that is surely the least of your concerns and mine too."

"Wait a minute, Sabina, how do you know anything about what's going on at Lakeview?"

"I don't know much, but I did ask Russ to keep an eye on Lakeview a while back.

"Sabina, I distinctly told you to keep away from that side of me until I am fully past it and can explain how dangerous it is."

"So you did. I'm sorry, Simon, but it started when you disappeared in August with no direct message. I am no mere hausfrau. I love you,

Simon, and when I fear you may have been taken into the evil bowels of whatever, it goads me into action."

"Well, it serves me right to fall in love with such a terrific modern woman."

"You got it. Anyway, Russ called me to alert me yesterday afternoon from his car phone. He said whatever was shaping up at Lakeview involved a whole bunch of agencies who have had Lakeview under surveillance and that it was lucky you weren't there. I haven't heard from him since. But the explosions there are all over the media."

"Shit, Sabina, you knew about all the surveillance?"

"Yes, I did."

"Why didn't you tell me?"

"Here we go again - you distinctly told me to keep out of it. My thinking was that it wasn't anything you didn't already know about. Was I wrong about that – that multiple surveillance operations surrounded the place?"

"Okay, you're right. I did know about that, but I thought, if anything, there were so many of them checking as much on each other that might keep the place safe."

"Well, I guess it didn't, and I don't know anything about that. So, what's next for you if you don't mind my interest as someone who loves you? What's to be done at this moment besides you coming back to me and allowing us to have a serious talk?"

"What do you mean?"

"Well, Simon, you are exposed to what happened in Philadelphia."

"How do you know about Philadelphia?"

"Russ went there too, and he knows more than you or any police force does about what happened there."

The phone connection was starting to break up. It was something about Russ knowing something or more than something about Philadelphia.

"I'm afraid that I may just have to turn myself over to the powers that be."

"We should meet with Russ before that - we can talk later about meeting with him. Simon. I love you so much."

He said, "I love you, Sabina," but the connection had broken off.

Simon sat in his car. Morning rush hour was at its peak, and he had to find a place to park and think through his options. He drove along Adelaide Street to a park that had an open parking space and pulled into it. He got out, walked over to a broken-down concrete bench, and sat down.

As he sat there, two police cars sped up and stopped.

He saw Chief of Detectives Colin Miservy heading his way.

"So, we've got you to ground."

"I didn't know you needed me again."

"We sure as hell do now. I came back to get you. Mind if I sit down?"

"Be my guest. It'll have to be on the collapsed part of the bench."

Miservy kept standing and waved away one of the police cars.

"Dr. Kiss, Simon, look, I don't know whether you know what happened at Lakeview – I understand you haven't been there since yesterday mid-afternoon."

"That is correct."

"Well, let me tell you of the events at Lakeview. I have never witnessed more happening in a few hours than what happened there last night."

Miservy filled Simon in on the waves of events that had occurred, including the apparently unintended Soviet agent deaths from fourth-party mortar fire. And then, later, Walker ordered even more explosions to support the joint military intelligence exercise story.

"Geez. I hope they didn't destroy my new trees."

"You serious? Anyway, everything on site is now under the protection of joint Canadian American military intelligence and connected to further Canadian police investigation related to multiple grievous deaths."

"Sounds pretty secure," said Simon, smiling weakly.

Miservy returned the weak smile. "I am afraid we are seeing worldwide television coverage of the first set of mortar explosions at Lakeview with all kinds of accompanying world media speculation. Perhaps it is fortunate that a seasoned three-star Lieutenant General from U.S. military intelligence has temporary control of the situation out there - the guy you work and worked for - Lamont Walker, whom some call 'Big.' He certainly is in more ways than one. Anyway, he obviously knows you quite well. He managed to convey the real events to the press with enough words to bury it for a while. The statement was read by the Canadian General heading up our military intelligence side."

Miservy read from a piece of paper,

"An event at this location occurred yesterday, filmed by unknown parties, that was a Canadian-American armed forces joint intelligence training exercise involving some live munitions to add realism to a simulation of circumstances such units might be expected to face in certain possible real situations. We might also state that closely analyzing the current media response is part of our training exercise."

Simon smiled at the last sentence – pure Big."

Miservy put aside the statement and said, "That Walker guy sure has balls."

"Yes, that was 'Big' Walker at his sly best. Indeed, I worked for him for three years. Anyway, where do I stand in all this? I mean, from your point of view, investigating some of the murders."

"Well, that remains a good question, for me at least. I mean, your computerized gaming certainly seems at the center of those murders and the events at Lakeview in the last 24 hours. Walker wants you out there now but also seems to trust me. It is certainly part of my inquiry to find out any further aspects of how you personally may be involved. I think the best way to proceed with you is to give you everything I have in hopes you give me everything you have and may be able to fill in some gaps."

"I would appreciate it if you would start," said Kiss.

"For starters, we have in custody out there two persons of very material interest. One is apparently your Soviet back-channel opposite, Ivan Tarasov."

"I do not deny I was working with Ivan. I'm not sure how much of that local police will be permitted to know, let alone reveal.

"Okay, agreed. Frankly, at this point, we can't disclose anything. The other guy is David Sommerfeld, a connected member of the American left whose group or whomever he reports to - he denies knowing who they are – and not whose cause he enlisted Martin Davies. However, he denies anything directly to do with Davies's murder. He is the guy the Philadelphia police are also seeking and may want to charge for the murder there that I was told you were also a person of interest or somehow involved you. I haven't heard that story yet. Finally, Sommerfeld also engineered the mortar bombardment last night to blow the cover of the back channel you and Tarasov are operating for the Pentagon. Sommerfeld says he only wanted to make your strategy gaming methods available for more than just military uses."

Simon was not very surprised. Sommerfeld had long been back-of-mind, and he had wondered when he would resurface. It was a compulsion of his to contact Sommerfeld every once in a while to keep him up to date on the state of computer-assisted strategic gaming and its potential for wider international policy application at some point when the methodology was no longer a defense secret. Indeed, he should have made clearer to Sommerfeld that his games in the arcade at Worlds and experimental work at the U of T, though still a military and trade secret, were paving the way for wider global policy applications, pushing a progressive cause further than he normally would. But he had only a vague memory of what all was said in those conversations.

When Miservy asked, Simon could only say he had last placed a call to Sommerfeld in August when he was in Montreal at Mirabel, but again couldn't recall what was said. He would now have to take those lapses more seriously and find some way to force himself to remember what seemed to be blocked in his mind. In the meantime, he knew he had to work something out with the police.

He finally told Miservy, "I am wondering what more I can provide you or the others about the deaths or other immediate events last night at and around my farm. After all, I wasn't present for any of it. And it seems you are one of a bunch of people picking up the pieces there last night who are now aware of what Ivan and I were doing out of Lakeview, as via the entertainment games at Worlds."

"Some general stuff was mentioned; I don't think anyone other than General Walker knows any of the specifics, even the CIA guy. Anyway, Walker wants me to find you and get you back there. Frankly, I'm prepared to take your word that you will remain around Toronto, with an immediate contact number pending further investigations. Also, I should tell you that we have a fourth murder or at least wrongful death– last night when Sommerfeld entered Lakeview, he disabled your houseman with a move he says he had been trained to do that was supposed to be non-lethal – your houseman never recovered consciousness and died from it, or at least that is the apparent cause of death."

"Cliff Forbes! Oh God…poor Cliff. That's terrible."

He held and shook his head back and forth in shock. "The Forbes are such a good and loyal couple. They have kept that farmhouse for decades. Do you know how Hilda, his wife, is taking it?"

"She is under sedation, but otherwise, I guess she will be alright. Look, I'm sure they would let you through to see her and observe the damage to your gardens from the mortar shelling and later staged explosions and by the clumping about of untold numbers of intruders, uniformed and un-uniformed."

"Hilda is made of strong stuff. The gardens are nothing to losing Cliff. I think Walker mainly wants to ball me out because he's pissed off and hasn't done so for a while. I'll go to the farm and debrief him and then get out of there until they're through. Otherwise, I'll be at my apartment or at Worlds. You have my phone numbers."

"Good. Walker said he would be at Lakeview until the end of the week. Otherwise, it would not look like a serious joint military forces operation. They are all pretending to measure stuff and take photos and walking around with clipboards, occasional jeeps bringing other brass in to inspect things – lots of good theatres. Walker's a genius if he can pull off the cover story. The reality is they are continuing to grill Tarasov. They gave us Sommerfeld and then sent me out to get you. So have fun out there."

"Okay."

"One last thing though, what the hell happened in Philadelphia? Their police are putting enormous pressure on you to at least interview you, and I can't hold them off much longer – they're sending a team up to talk to you."

"Can you wait a day or so on that? I know how I might find out more about that. The short of it is that I was there very briefly at Mathematics Trust the day of the death and heard two people arguing on the floor above but left just before whatever bad happened."

"I hope you can make that credible."

"Yes, so do I."

Miservy said, "Good. I trust you."

"Takes two - I trust you too. Thanks for going easy with me right now."

Miservy went to his car and was driven away.

Simon remained on the bench. A disheveled guy came over to him asking for money. He gave the guy $5, got up, and headed for Lakeview.

Chapter 31

At Lakeview, Simon made his way through the various security cordons and entered his home.

Walker had taken over the conservatory as his command post. He looked up at Simon and said, "About time you got here. Take a seat."

"Lovely space you got here, Big."

"Don't start with me. Why the hell were you at a Halloween party last night and not here where you were supposed to be."

"I had a good costume?"

"Godamn it, there you go again with the jokes."

"Well, I did. The short answer was that it was too big an event, and I was too central to it to miss. Ivan and I had everything set up to complete our runs and report to you by the end of today. We can still do so now, so by the end of today, if you let me return with him to Worlds. Where is he?"

"He's upstairs, but wait a minute – what do you know about what happened here last night? That guy Sommerfeld you know, was central to it! The police have him now, and he's committed numerous crimes."

"Yeah, I heard – Miservy came to see me. I'm confined to this area indefinitely while all that is investigated. I don't know a damn thing about what he was up to or what happened here last night. Nothing."

"You don't get away that easily. He said you talked to him on the phone lots of times."

"Yes, that is my one vulnerability. I don't remember those calls in any detail, except they were generally about putting my system to work for non-military uses. It is an idea we shared, just not as fast as he seemed to think feasible. I don't know anything about him in recent years, otherwise."

"You better not. What about the death in Philly – you on the hook for that?"

"Miservy says a team of their detectives will be up here in the next day or so to interview me. I think I can explain everything to their satisfaction."

"Hmm. Anyway, the damage here is done. The notion we're doing some kind of back-channel stuff with the Russians is all over the media and had got me into deep doo-doo in Washington. Looks to me Sommerfeld at least got his wish to disrupt our little game. When I get back, there'll be some kind of reckoning, and you will likely have to come down there to help me explain the limited nature of the information flow into and out of the back channel feeding each side's still very secure war gaming."

"My admiration for your doing what we did knows no bounds. I will certainly stand up for you."

"Good. So, return to work with Ivan downstairs, I guess. I'll continue to enjoy the view up here."

"Please do so. Drinks are in the cabinet. Piano's out of tune, though."

"Get the hell out of my sight."

For the rest of the day, Simon and Ivan completed their final report on the back game results. It could only stress the need for even greater caution because of the destabilizing bipolar nature of the current American and Soviet leadership and show the need to restrain Star Wars initiatives and announcements or face Soviet "incidents." Not much of a surprise, given the scene at Lakeview and sensational speculation in the media.

Later that night, Simon returned to his apartment at the Four Seasons. He was eager to see Sabina. Before he could call her, he received a call from Russell that he would like to see him and Sabina the next day. When he called Sabina, it was arranged the three would meet for lunch at Simon's apartment the next day.

Sabina and Russell arrived together at noon.

Simon embraced Sabina. She said, "God, Simon, I hope you are out of any danger. What a mess at Lakeview."

"I think things have righted themselves as far as I'm concerned. The prospect is I'm through with the military and free to live a full life up here."

"Well, I'm here to share with you some photos I have."

They went into the kitchen, where Simon had eggs and fixings out to make omelets. They sat down at the big table.

"Okay," he said, "so, Russ, what's this all about?"

Sabina said, "I asked Russ to go down to Philadelphia to sniff around the Mathematics Trust…."

"What! Sabina, I told you don't get involved in my risky stuff."

"Okay. Okay, I thought it was background and might connect with whomever seems to spook you from your past. Certainly, nothing connected with recent events up here. Incredibly, Russ was down there the same day you were, much to our surprise."

"Oh, geez, Sabina."

"It's enough to get you off the hook. Here are the dated and timed photos I took, in sequence, from when I got there around 4:15 that afternoon to when the cops arrived at 5:30ish. The first one is of a guy looking out an upstairs back window. 4:46."

"My god, that's Sommerfeld."

"Yes, and then, the next photos are of you, twenty minutes later, entering and leaving the place over a period of just over five minutes. I didn't realize that was you until Sabina told me. If I had known that was you, I would have gone to you first."

"I'm surprised you didn't recognize me."

"Sorry, I'm not a member at Worlds."

"Well, I'm sorry you're so disadvantaged. I did here you attended Upper Canada College."

"Yes, I had a rich aunt who paid for that. It gave me my entre among the uppers, plus a good training in chutzpah."

"I'm sure you're kept quite busy. Anyway, I went in that day because the Board was going to wind up the Trust, and I thought I'd drop off a cheque that might keep it going. But I heard the argument going on upstairs, and one voice was Sommerfeld - I knew his voice. As I piece it together, the other guy must have been the Trust's lawyer – the subsequent possible murder victim. If it's murder, what I can't put together is Sommerfeld's motive – I mean, he is far too analytic to kill somebody emotionally, let alone someone he already knew and who merely took financial advantage of him when he was the Director of the Trust.

"There's got to be either more to it or less – such as the guy fell down the stairs accidentally in their scuffle- but who's going to believe Sommerfeld, especially now? Anyway, it seems the police down there have since found out that the FBI connected Sommerfeld with Martin Davies up here. And that went to me because we had all been at Penn together, and that connected because Davies and I received their awards at about the same time. They seem to have concluded, without any prodding from the FBI, that we three are all tied together in murders there and here and likely on the wrong side of the Cold War."

"Any connection to me, even as you witnessed it, that's accidental both down there and up here. Fortunately, the Toronto police think so too. But if the police get these photos, they'll say five minutes was plenty of time for me to have been involved in that lawyer's death."

"So, you want me to withhold the photos?"

"No. You and I will go to Miservy and will have to take an interview with the Philadelphia police. The fact is I knew nothing about the lawyer in question down there or any connection he may have had with Sommerfeld or with the Mathematics Trust. I just went in intending to leave the envelope with my cheque and the note with it – which I still have, by the way - and leave.

I was being interviewed without notice by the CIA about the Keefe death and related disturbance at Worlds before I was driven to Philadelphia to spend a ten-hour plane delay at my old haunts at Penn. I only decided on the spot to go to West Philly. My CIA driver will vouch for that. Anyway, I think I'll be okay, although now I'm concerned that they will question Russ about how he came to be there at the same time I was."

"I'll just say I'm on retainer as your private investigator and thought I should brush up on your past in Philadelphia. No need to bring Sabina into it."

Simon frowned. "But you're on retainer with the Hursts, not me. They chose to include me in your activity, including keeping a watch on Lakeview. See, it's going to get back to Sabina wanting you to go down there and her suspicions about my past."

Sabina said, "I think the three of us should go to the police. I don't think there's any way around it, Simon. I sensed you were troubled by your past and wanted to know why. It seemed to be about or at least started with your Philadelphia period at Penn. I had the means to do some sleuthing and did so via Russ. Let's get it all out. And end it. Period. I do silly things like that because I love you, damn it. What say you, Simon, Russ?"

Russ said, "I agree - straightforward is best. They will try to pry other stuff out of me, but the fact is there's nothing else they can get from me or Sabina."

Simon thought about it.

"Okay, you're right. But you better both be ready to be pestered for a while about this, including even by the news media. They will collectively smell a rat, I'm sure, though none is there in Philly, at least."

Russ said, "Well, I've been through extreme media pressure several times, so it's kind of old hat to me. What about you, Sabina?"

"We ladies love to wear a new hat."

Simon said, "Very funny, Sabina, my love, but I suspect that this is one new hat you may be glad to get rid of.

Later that night, Sabina pressed Simon about the detail of his past which still nagged at her.

"Simon, there's something that doesn't add up to me. I can't figure out your relationship over the years with David Sommerfeld. I mean, you sometimes talk about it as not even being able to remember your contacts with him."

"It's something I don't myself understand. I mean, I agree with his goal of making use of policy simulation gaming internationally on issues other than war gaming. But that's not on yet, not during another hot period in the Cold War. And whenever I have talked to him over the years, my mind seems to block most of it afterward."

"This may seem whacky, but do you think that he may have some kind of hypnotic effect on you."

"Believe it or not, you're not the first one to suggest that. But I have always been the one to initiate contact – that part I remember except for the contact we had back as students at Penn. We met several times the week after the car accident. I was wandering around in kind of a daze that week."

"Yes, you told me it was traumatic for you."

"I guess. The only thing I can clearly remember from that week in Philadelphia was that there were several huge thunderstorms."

"Well, if you can't remember, I'm not too surprised. I think you should avoid contact with Sommerfeld from now on. Should be easy - after all, he may be headed for jail."

"You're probably right, though I would prefer to face him head-on about this at some point."

"Well, um, let's get some sleep."

She pecked at him some more.

Pecking became love-making.

After that, they agreed, "God, it was good," and faded into sleep.

Chapter 32

Miservy had come to Simon, Russell, and Sabina the next day at Simon's apartment. He was surprised at what he learned from them but again trusted what he heard.

"I'll arrange for you to talk to the Philadelphia police. I'll be there to support you to the extent they will give me any . Whatever they conclude, I doubt they can't get Simon away from here without approval from higher American federal authority. In the circumstances, I doubt that will be forthcoming. In the meantime, Walker is still holding Sommerfeld, and we have to go out there with Simon to decide what happens next with him. My hope is that he may just release Sommerfeld to us for prison and criminal prosecution here.

Miservy and Simon drove out the following morning. It was still very much General Walker's show at Lakeview. He began, "I think we finally have all the living principals here in the room to make a decision about Sommerfeld. Proceed, Detective Chief Miservy, please."

Miservy said, "We know that Martin Davies had sent a statement in a confidential note first to warn his Minister, Mike Keefe. It admits Davies' foolish contacts with Sommerfeld and that he knew nothing of Sommerfeld's mysterious network other than foolishly sharing its apparent "progressive" objectives. Keefe was just getting that in hand when he was murdered at Worlds, an accidental victim apparently intended to be Davies.

Miservy continued, "I doubt any of that other than naming Sommerfeld will give us anything. Davies received instructions from Sommerfeld from untraceable phone numbers over the last few months. Sommerfeld here, in turn, has a record of only one of his phone calls and can identify no-one with the group he reported to. The network of top people who sucked Sommerfeld and then Davies in to save the world was extremely careful about remaining unknown to those who worked for them."

Sommerfeld added, "Industrial espionage goes on all the time, and I didn't know until very recently that Simon. Kiss was still actively involved in an American military back game with the Soviets."

"Well, there, you've nailed it," said Warrington. "The President is aware of what's happened here and wants our report. He's already apparently chased your Chief of General Staff out of the Oval Office."

"Damn it, Warrington, the back games are too big for just the CIA, even the President. For three years now, they have been an essential part of how we think about nuclear war and for some of us in the Pentagon, and that means how to avoid it in the first place, especially in hot periods like now."

Simon held a finger out. "In fact, it was because of the destabilization findings emerging in the latest back game compared to 1980 that led me to ensure I had enough left at Worlds in case of any self-destruct at Lakeview. That's now been reported to General Walker.

Miservy said, "Okay, that part is up to General Walker from now on."

Sommerfeld kept muttering, "I am too smart to have been so naïve. It is unforgivable...."

Simon said, "You know, David, I know other very smart people who are naïve. Davies was obviously one. Especially if they can imagine a better world and the means they think can attain it."

Walker said, "You big thinkers are more interested in ideas than people. Right, Sommerfeld? A neat idea, thus saving the world; who cares if it involves a few people dead to get things rolling? Shit..."

Miservy said, "With respect, General Walker, one shouldn't badger the witness."

"Witness! This guy isn't just a witness – he's one of the perps, as far as I can see. Just maybe not the top guy."

"As far as we know at this point, Sommerfeld did not do, authorize, or know in advance about the Toronto killings, and the death in Philadelphia was plausibly accidental. The three KGB were entirely a surprise to him."

Warrington said, "Yeah, the sale of the farm east of Lakeview is being investigated."

"Well, Sommerfeld and his excessive idealism sure as hell aided and abetted those deaths too."

Warrington said, "So, Miservy, why did you bring Simon Kiss here today? You could have shared new facts without him here."

Miservy replied, "I wanted him and Sommerfeld face to face for a moment, with witnesses."

He turned to Simon.

"And now that you're here, and we are all in absolute confidence, here I will ask Simon: how do we know Rondo itself is secure at Worlds? I would have sent a team in to get it, but it's surrounded with press these days."

"It is secure, for now, it better be, or it will take me at least a year to reconstruct it. The "Mr. X" breach at Worlds the night of Keefe's death will not be repeated. I already eliminated from my system any record of the latest back game. It only now exists as we reported on its nuclear stability implications."

Simon looked severely at Sommerfeld.

Sommerfeld said, "T may have suggested I knew enough about what you were building here that with my help it could be replicated. But I never gave them any of that information, and when Davies was murdered decided I never would, only pretend to be ready to do so until I could identify who they were."

Walker said, "Someone unidentified we know only as 'Mr. X' was in the arcade as a guest of the oil guys the night Mike Keeve was killed. Do you have any idea who that might be – I mean, there's the oil connection?"

"None whatsoever. Their operations or operatives up here other than me and Davies were unknown to me. But I now wouldn't doubt it was likely the network I'm ignorant of and unfortunately involved with."

Tarasov muttered, "Still a mess," and then added more audibly, "I expect to have a further word with some or all the agencies here. Frankly, I will need protection. The KGB never forgives. I cannot go back to the Soviet Union now. I will have to live over here."

Walker shrugged. "If you continue to reside in Canada, the Canadians will have to do the protecting. I mean, the Canadian authorities have taken care of the dead KGB. They have gotten word through to the KGB that maybe their three guys got dead from a fourth-party "peacenik" operation that went awry. Maybe they will believe enough of that to clear Tarasov."

"Never," said Ivan.

Walker said, "Anyway, we ask here that the police investigation of Sommerfeld and resulting charges make public the motive that any attempted theft of the Rondo tape was motivated for commercial advantage with no reference to any military and intelligence implications. The commercial motive will be believable, and it does not alter Sommerfeld's guilt or not of the crimes he may have committed, including the possibility of murder charges."

Simon said, "I hope that works with the media."

"Yes, we local police agree with that," said Miservy. I cannot guarantee what the prosecution will pursue, but that seems easiest for them. Otherwise, everything is tied up in various security and intelligence squabbles. Indeed, that may even be the truth of the matter?"

Simon remained silent. "You got that right," said Walker

Miservy resumed. "There's one more thing I want to pursue a bit with both Sommerfeld and Simon in the same room, with witnesses. Sommerfeld, can you tell us about the phone calls you received from Simon from time to time?"

"Sure. They were odd. Simon would call, and we would always start by agreeing on the need for non-military progressive uses of his Rondo set-up – for wider conflict resolution around the world and global policy development gaming. Then Simon would urge me to do whatever I could to speed that up. He would stress that. On a few calls, he even fed me some stuff he was doing with his Rondo set-up. I never knew quite what to make of those calls over the years. Even one from Mirabel the very night Keefe was killed."

There was uneasiness around the room as everyone looked at Simon.

"Miservy said, "Simon, tell us what you said in these calls."

"I can't; I mean, I can't recall anything but the first part- agreeing on progressive uses of the Rondo gaming platform."

Walker exclaimed, "Jesus. This is news to me. What the hell did you spill to him about the back channel?"

Sommerfeld quickly said, "There was never anything about that, only 'non-military uses."

Miservy said, "Simon, can you swear you didn't egg on Sommerfeld and even his group to get at your Rondo thing?"

Simon bent his head, with his fingers on his brow, and finally said, "No, they are a complete blank after the first part of the conversations."

Miservy said firmly, "Simon, somehow, you're going to have to summon up those phone conversations. For Walker's sake and intelligence agencies first, but most assuredly for your own sake in the criminal investigations and pending court cases."

"Yes…," was all Simon could say.

Walker said, "You got that right," and strode out, leaving Simon wondering if and hoping himself, that would be the last time they saw each other as one working for the other.

Chapter 33

Two days later, Simon received the difficult news that David Sommerfeld had committed suicide in jail. Simon presumed it was because of Sommerfeld's remorse over the several deaths he had been associated with, even if indirectly or without his intent. Perhaps even more remorse at his naïve idealism that had stupidly led to those grievous results.

Simon was doubly distressed with the news because he would now never be able to discuss his own past mysterious contacts with Sommerfeld over the years since his university. He would now have to resort to other methods of understanding and recovering his lost memory of those contacts,

Anatol Rapoport was back in his University of Toronto office in the Sydney Smith Building, down the hall from the Psychology Department. He had just returned from a quick visit to Vienna. He looked up and saw Simon entering his office. He gave Simon a big smile.

"Great to see you, Simon - I almost think of you as my son."

"In a way, I am – son of you and the likes of Tom Schelling, Ken Boulding, Herb Simon, and the other great post-war strategic behavior cum moral thinkers in the social sciences.

"Maybe not Herb, on the moral thing. But I see in the media that there were fireworks at Lakeview the other night. I'm glad I was out of the country, given my part out there, small as it was. I also just heard about David Sommerfeld's suicide. Very sad."

"Yes. A sometime friend. Alas, not before gave a good lead on my connection with all of that to the police. Anyway, Anatol, your part was important for me, both reminding me of my conscience and on the technical side of dealing with bimodality. You are, of course, in no way associated with the deaths and destruction out there, r in the city."

"All part of your checking me out as a security risk while consulting my technical expertise?"

"Yes, and now I need to seek out some more of your expertise."

"What's that?"

"You talked to me a bit about my past and the fact that I could not remember my contacts with David Sommerfeld over the years since Penn."

"Vividly. I mentioned that you might need some help with that."

"Anatol, I need to recover those memories. I am now convinced that somehow not entirely consciously, I too may have helped make some of these bad things happen."

"Well, that might have been a subconscious process. To me, you may have been so distraught at the death of Donna Meyer back in Penn days that you may have suffered a psychotic episode.

Simon looked uneasily at Rapaport.

Rapaport said, "As we agreed, one good approach to this might be hypnosis. Curt Ansfer is a professor of Psychiatry here. His main office is at the Clarke Institute, but he shares a small office in this building, and I think he may be there now. He employs hypnosis in his clinical practice, and I'm sure I could arrange an appointment for you."

"That sounds interesting. I would like to meet with him. Thanks, Anatol."

"He ducked in a few minutes before you did to say hello. Let's see if he's still there."

The two men went down the hall and were welcomed into Ansfer's office. He was a big man, nearly bald, and otherwise met the stereotype of a psychiatrist: he wore a three-piece tweedy suit and had a full black beard and mustache and heavy-rimmed glasses. He smiled as he was introduced to Simon.

"Happy to meet you, Dr. Kiss – you are sometimes in the news."

"Reluctantly, I assure you."

"I do have a few moments. Sit down." He pointed to two chairs and cleared some of the piles of books and papers on his cluttered desk.

"We come in strict confidence, Curt. Simon has explained to me a problem that may have had as its cause an event or events earlier in his life. Recovering his memory of that and his memory of certain succeeding events may well respond to your methods. So, I have brought him here to you. I will let you two discuss things and will withdraw."

After Rapoport left, Kiss filled in Ansfer about the trauma he had experienced at Penn, shared by a sympathetic Sommerfeld, and Simon's occasional and hazy contacts with Sommerfeld ever since. And the fact that he could not now review that with Sommerfeld.

Ansfer listened carefully with his hands folded.

"Why does that trouble you – has it occurred to you that you could just leave it in the past?"

"Those moments of vaguely recalled contact have recurred, even quite recently. I don't know why. Also, it may have led to things and events that I never consciously intended or foresaw. It may even have indirectly contributed to the Ontario government murders still being investigated, though I mention that in strict confidence."

"No worry about that. And those are two unsettling reasons to keep working at what you can't remember. Are you aware of the methods of hypnosis?"

"Not really, but I'm willing to try just about anything to recover those lost memories."

"Well, hypnosis largely requires a willing patient. I have had very few successes with unwilling patients – that is, unwilling to remember and report on something they regard as destructive of their self-definition. In your case, you are smart and confident enough likely to be flexible about your self-image. But equally, you are likely among the smartest patients I will ever have, and overall, I have found that smart critical minds have trouble truly losing conscious control to a hypnotic state. And most importantly, I must warn you, as with any psychiatric procedure: the most successful results may be very disturbing to anyone whose psyche may have taken such elaborate measures to suppress certain things."

"Well, I'm willing to try, and on my dime, please."

"You may not want an accounting trail. Let's just proceed and see about such things later. I have a slot for you tomorrow afternoon after 3:00 - is that possible for you?"

"I'll make it possible. Thank you for seeing me."

"Let's keep using my office here."

"Yes. It's a date."

Simon slipped into a parking spot just before 3:00 the next afternoon. He had talked it through with Sabina and spent a restless night thinking about Dr. Ansfer's cautionary remarks about even the successful use of hypnosis.

He knocked, and to Ansfer's "Come," he again entered the small office and took one of the chairs.

Ansfer began, "First, let's have a little more of your background. The highlights will be fine."

Simon gave him some details, including again the dramatic events of his student life at Penn, and concluded, "I grew up with great advantages; after that, perhaps partly because I was from a wealthy Jewish family with high expectations for its son, I have worked hard to make use of my advantages. From time to time, I felt, well, I have felt a little guilty about my advantages. I can't rid myself of the thought there's an equally undeserved stain running through my life."

The answer made a few notes and looked up. "A stain? Could you tell me some more about those feelings?"

"I just…I just think I've come up short in giving something back. I mean, I'm not a practicing Jew, but I agree with Jewish humanism – a man has a duty to his fellow man, the more so when you are as advantaged as I have been."

"Would you say those guilt feelings are powerful within you?"

"Yes, since my university days."

"What happened there specifically to give you such a sense of guilt?"

"I guess two things, close together. I was at a party with other university students one night, and the David Sommerfeld, whom I mentioned, went off on a tirade about students who didn't have to face the struggles of most students – students who were "favored" to use his words and hadn't really faced any tests yet. Everyone knew he was talking about me. Apparently, at that time, he was openly envious of me.

"Then, as I mentioned, the girl I had fallen for at the time was killed in a car accident. Actually, we had had our first sex the day before she left. Davies used to call me Canada Dry because I had gone along with her on not having sex until we were more sure of each other. I didn't know until later she was doing it with another guy. She told me that last day, "We're good forever, let's do it." When I was rolling on a safe, she said, "No, do it bare bone - who cares if we have a kid?" I couldn't resist. We jumped on each other and stayed on each other for a good part of the afternoon.

Ansfer made a few notes and glanced at Simon to continue.

"Anyway, the next day, she left on a trip south to Duke University. I had encouraged her to go on, to encourage her interest in physics. I found out after the accident that she was traveling with some pretty rough Yippie types to do some anti-war action, not to attend the conference we had agreed she would. I came to realize that she had not told me some stuff about herself. Someone I trusted told me she had thought people who weren't rich, like her family, were kind of useless in the scheme of things.

"Then, David Sommerfeld had lunch with me a few times in the week following her death and sort of made me feel better – that I was okay and contributing to good causes. I guess that was the first time with him that I can't really remember any of the details. The main thing I can remember was that it was a very stormy week in Philadelphia after Donna was killed."

"You mean the weather?"

"Yes. There was some local flooding."

The Ansfer made another note.

"Okay, that's all the time I have today. Could you come in the same time, the day after tomorrow?"

"I'll make the time."

"Good."

Two days later, their conversation resumed.

"Today, I'd like you to recall as much as you can about the subsequent contacts you had with Sommerfeld."

"In chronological order?"

"Any way you wish to go through them."

"Well, I can remember at least one phone call I made to a number - I kept getting mail notification of a change in his number. That was the last year I was in California – 1978. I couldn't hear him well over the phone because of repeated cracks of thunder outside, but again I was in a low mood and was feeling very stressed about my decision to go to Washington to help them develop their war gaming. I only recall that he seemed to soothe me and ask me some questions. But I can't remember any details. I cannot remember what I said."

Ansfer completed a note.

"When was the next contact?" for a bit

"There weren't many when I moved to Washington because my phones were tapped. But I recall being in a restaurant in Alexandria one night, though - it was St. Patrick's Day, and a bunch of us went there for green beer through a helluva thunderstorm when I temporarily misplaced my briefcase. I think I made a call from the restaurant phone that night, but once again, I can't remember any details – I don't even know whom I called that night, but I do vaguely remember it forwarded a bit to other numbers, which began to annoy me. I have a vaguer recollection of other calls before or after that. It was the same thing with the last call I made to him. It was late August. My flight from San Francisco to Toronto went through a severe wind shear going through a storm front, and we were re-routed to Mirabel in Montreal. I had to wait the rest of the night for the storms to go through Montreal. I was in another sort of trance for a bit."

"You realized that?'

"Sort of. Anyway, I believe I made some calls from a phone box at Mirabel that night, but I can't remember anything else about that night except I un-expectantly met a business friend who had attended the same conference in San Francisco. That part is clear. I had recently learned my great aunt was ailing. I used that as an excuse and stayed in Montreal for a few days, using the opportunity to meet her and to meet my business friend the next night. After three days in Montreal, I got back to Toronto and Worlds, where some hell had broken out."

"The death of Michael Keefe?"

"Yes."

The Ansfer looked over his notes and was silent for a while.

Finally, he said,

"What you have described may correspond to a series of psychotic episodes – indeed, episodes in which you may have even temporarily dissociated from your normal psyche and acted in a way that is not your normal self, even the opposite of your normal self."

"My god, Ansfer, do I have a split personality?"

"Maybe, to some extent, and at certain rare times, though obviously most of the time not to the point of a threat to the functioning of your normal self. Regarding the rare times, there does seem to be one specific pattern."

"What's that," said Simon, only slightly relieved.

"There is usually a trigger for such episodes. In your case, each of the episodes you have described was apparently accompanied by and, therefore, possibly triggered by severe thunderstorms and likely a sudden drop in atmospheric pressure as part of the storm system – a low-pressure area moving through with a big frontal change in weather. I can check the atmospheric pressure of the week in Philadelphia, I think, in the Washington D.C. area on that St Patrick's day and last August when that big storm system moved through the mid-west and south-eastern Canada."

"My God, could something as simple as weather change my whole personality?"

"Well, let's not jump to conclusions. Our next meeting will prepare us for hypnotic therapy. As a first step, I want you to relax and stare at this swinging watch."

Simon tried to completely relax and thought he had done so.

Ansfer looked at Kiss and again started swinging his pocket watch. It went back and forth for a while. It gradually lost momentum. Then it came to a stop.

"So," said Simon, "does that turn me into a hypnotic?"

"Not in your case. I am not surprised you will be a difficult subject. It will be necessary to begin with self-hypnosis. We will get to that next time. You may find that very helpful in heading off future episodes as well as a possible first step in entering the deeper hypnosis necessary to activate and then face your suppressed memories."

Ansfer looked at his daily journal and said, "Shall we meet again, same time, in two days?"

"Yes, for sure."

Two days later, Simon entered Ansfer's office in a tense state. He wasn't sure what was about to happen, and that bothered him. Also, a severe low-pressure storm system was passing through, and he had already learned that it could threaten his mental stability.

Ansfer greeted him and said, "I see you are tense today. My barometer tells me you may be close to the conditions that may trigger your mental abnormality if we are right about the trigger mechanism. In fact, these are ideal conditions for beginning your training in self-hypnotism."

"You seem set on this self-hypnotism – why not just try ordinary hypnotism?"

"I have already concluded that that alone will not work in your case. I am going to have to rely on your own auto-suggestion as a first stage before we need to try other hypnotic techniques. You will have to develop your own therapy after that. These are not pleasant memories you may be dealing with. It will be necessary to recover and feed them through several mental defense levels before you can accept them at the conscious level."

"Alright. Please proceed."

"The first requirement is that you relax, as deeply as possible, in your conscious state. I would like you to sit back and form an enclosed shape by joining your thumbs and index fingers like this. I want you to look through that shape at the blank wall behind me, to my left. Take a moment. What shape do you see – for example, is it circular?"

"No, it's more like a circus tent - straight bottom, with a top that has a bit of a curve."

"Good, now I want you to consider the space made by your fingers to be a space that is empty. I want you to let go of all your thoughts until your only thought is the shape of that space. Take your time."

"What are your thoughts now," Ansfer said a few minutes later.

"I still see a circus tent. There's a storm outside, but we're safe inside, and everyone is laughing at the clowns."

"I want you to let go of any thoughts about that space.

He waited a moment.

"Now, it can be a very agreeable space because when you imagine something in it, it represents a good moment from your childhood when all was safe and desirable. You will be more and more relaxed there. Keep looking at the space. That's right. Relax now and enjoy being in that space – there is nothing in there hurting you or threatening you. The storm is scary, but it is outside."

After a few minutes more of Ansfer's calm encouragement, Simon felt unusually relaxed and had become transfixed by the "empty" space he was looking at through the frame shaped by his hands.

"Now I want you to put into that space a thought about how you are going to completely unlock the mysteries of your past in the storms with David Sommerfeld."

After a while, Simon spoke very clearly, "That circus I loved as a child has a succession of rings and acts. The obstacle course at Worlds came to mind. I will take the obstacle course at Worlds – each obstacle has a choice. I will make the hardest choice at each obstacle, and that will bring forth those suppressed memories. Then I will remember, and then I will deal with them."

It took a few minutes for Simon to come fully out of his self-hypnotic state.

"Ansfer?" he said. "I must have just undergone hypnotherapy. I am a little dizzy."

"That's normal. And I think you have auto-suggested a most interesting exercise to bring forth your suppressed memories. Do you recall your proposal?"

"Ah, the last thing I really remember was the shape of the space between my thumbs and the bent fingers above them. It was a sort of - gosh, I've already forgotten. No, wait, it looked like the shape of a circus tent."

"Yes, you brought forward a good memory from your childhood. You must have enjoyed your visits to the circus in childhood.

"Yes, yes, I did, actually. So much of it astonished me. Nothing much else did."

"So, Simon, I believe this was a successful session. You went through self-hypnosis first by staring into the shape made by your folded fingers. Your mind brought forth a circus tent. And the succession of circus rings. That made you available to my suggestion to find your own way through to your suppressed memories. In fact, you have proposed to put yourself through the obstacle course at Worlds such that at each obstacle, you choose the most difficult option, and in so doing, during the subsequent exertion, you summon forth the suppressed memories of your contacts with Sommerfeld over the years."

"Yes, yes, I did."

"What you have proposed, I believe, will be a very effective convergence of physical and mental effort. In fact, it is a brilliant solution to your problem, which I could never have imagined myself or drawn from you with other hypnotherapy. I *w*ant you to put it into effect as soon as possible."

"Did I actually suggest all that?"

"You did, Simon."

"My God, thank you very much. Could it really work like that?"

"I'm not sure it will, though you seemed very committed to it. Also, though, I think it wise for me to be there at the obstacle course. It could involve severe mental shocks to you."

Chapter 34

For the next few days, Simon pondered whether he should try his own self-hypnotically devised test at Worlds.

Dr. Ansfer had said that Simon should not discuss it with others, including Sabina. He had said, "It is your test for you alone at this point. It could only weaken your inner resolve if others, however well intended, interfere with it or complicate it. You must be under your own self-command as you go through the obstacle course, or the inner secrets you are blocking will not come free."

Simon didn't know how much longer he could withhold it from Sabina. That had prompted him to decide a time at the club when Terry Moon, the Fitness Director, could make sure Simon was the only one using the obstacle course.

At 10:00 on a Tuesday morning, Simon approached the first stage of the obstacle course. He knew that each of the four stages had an option between an easier and a harder type of obstacle test, such that the total course had eight possible ways to go through it.

He had gone through it many times, but he had never chosen the more difficult of the two options at every stage. Only good athletes could do that well. He held a club record for one of the sequences he did well, but he was not likely to get close to the few super-people who chose the most difficult challenge through all four stages.

This time, however, would be different. He had set his course to go through the most difficult options so that the physical pressure of doing that would psychically break through his mental block about his unremembered contacts with Sommerfeld. All he could do was breathe in deeply and hope the physical strategy and his physical capacity to achieve it would work on and set free his blocked mental state.

The first set of obstacles presented a choice between a two-rope swing of twenty-five feet or a stomp through a 12-foot circle of eight moving tire treads that moved at different speeds. He chose the more difficult tire test. He was stabilizing into the third set of moving tires when it started to happen – he saw Donna Mayer's face in a car window beside his own. She smiled and waved at him. He veered a bit both in his brief memory flash and on the tires.

He raised his knees higher and put in all the energy he had left into getting across the variably moving tire field. But his astonishing recollection the moment before caused him to trip on the second last tire set. He finally regained his balance on the last tire set. Even as he did so, he recalled an early call from Sommerfeld: "At Penn in our last year, you and Davies made a commitment to me to participate in a future project. I am that project, Simon. You must keep in contact with me in times like this. You must give me all the information I ask you for to assist the future project." He gave Simon a phone number and said that Simon could contact him whenever he felt the need and that the number would be periodically updated.

Simon was astonished at how clearly he now recalled that exchange. Sommerfeld had given him a long-distance phone number with an "area code." Had that been some sort of further hypnotic suggestion when Simon was in a weak mental state? He stood at the end of the tire obstacle. He recalled Sommerfeld had taken psychology all the way through his undergraduate years. Hence, then, Sommerfeld's clever statements at the party about someone very much resembling Simon not having been truly 'tested' yet as had other less fortunate students at Penn.

But the mental distraction of all this recall led Simon to stumble out of the obstacle onto the floor, and he badly bruised his shoulder. He had no time to gather himself before the next choice of obstacles presented itself: a very taxing run on a fast treadmill versus a tricky climbing wall with changing footholds. He again chose the most difficult option and grappled his way onto and up the climbing wall.

Midway through this second obstacle test, his mind regained memory of his next phone contacts with Sommerfeld in the middle and late 1970s. He had initiated the calls to Sommerfeld at his ever-changing phone numbers. He now realized he had told Sommerfeld details of his evolving Rondo strategy gaming system and told him that he had been approached by the Pentagon to head up the war gaming work there. He would consider making a generous financial contribution to Sommerfeld's mysterious new 'group' to do wonders in the world. He had never followed through on the financial contribution. But how could he have forgotten this? Simon came to fully consider that he was fighting an intermittently split personality. He thought, "Where is this leading, and what else has the 'other me' done?"

As Simon wondered at his recovering past, he slipped on the wall and bloodied his right elbow. He painfully redoubled his efforts to get to the top of the wall and then dropped back down. Once again, he had no time to think about anything other than his next choice on the obstacle course.

He figured, with his bruises and cuts on his arms and shoulder, that the next choice would be obvious: a hurdle run, which he had managed a few times without hitting a hurdle, or duck walk courses. Both headed halfway back to the beginning of the obstacle course, where he could exit to the showers and change rooms. He chose the duckwalk. He pushed his way through chains and then through mud under low branches until he fell exhausted.

There, Simon experienced his final and most deeply repressed memory of Donna – her smile vanishing. He was in the passing lane trying to stay abreast of the car she was a backseat passenger in. He wanted them to pull over – he wanted to persuade her to return to Philadelphia. He didn't intend to, but his car crowded hers. It veered off the road at an overpass. He looked behind and saw the fiery explosion when it hit an overpass pier. But he continued for ten minutes to the next interchange with a sudden new thought: I must return to Philadelphia; Donna is waiting for me. I must try to accept her leftist causes. Northbound again, he had passed without slowing many emergency vehicles at the scene of a terrible accident, traffic already backed up endlessly in the southbound lanes.

Now, as those terrible memories flowed back into his conscious self, he cried out in horror. He was weeping as he finally was able to stand. He staggered off the obstacle course and along to the mirrored hallway that headed toward the changing rooms. He sank onto a bench, exhausted, hurting, mud-splattered, trying to bear still unbearable grief.

As if to push it all away, he dove into a lap pool at the end of the course. It forced him to swim against a very strong current for 100 feet. His angle had been wrong, and he had hit his head on the side. He was now bloodied and bruised on several parts of his body but dizzy from the head bash. He forced himself to the end of the pool and managed to grab the rope, and climbed out of the pool.

He felt his way along the mirrored hallway leading to the change rooms but fell to a kneeling position and stared at himself in the mirror, his head now ringing and clanging with shattering noise.

He gripped his head and nodded back and forth until his scream became audible, and he smashed his head into the mirror with such force that it cracked all over and prevented him from seeing himself except as some horrible distortion of humanity.

"That bastard! You bastard! THAT BASTARD IS YOU!"

He repeated, "That bastard is you!" over and over again at his twisted image in the mirror, pounding his fist against the now shattering glass, cutting into his hands.

Until Sabina ran up to him and took him from the mirror, and cradled him in her lap.

Moon and Ansfer were just behind her. Ansfer yelled, "Simon, you have regained yourself. That bastard is gone! You have begun to heal yourself."

Sabina hugged him strongly. "Oh, my love, let me wipe away the blood. We'll find the real bastard behind all this."

Part Six:
December 1983

Chapter 35

The fact was that Sabina did love to sleuth. She had personally arranged Russell's investigative work in Philadelphia. Now, as Simon hopefully recovered from the trauma of recovering his full self, She decided to look into something else in Simon's background that he had touched on in recalling other things in the weeks since. He had recalled that Sommerfeld was not the only one who may have envied Simon at Penn – another "big" guy always seemed to be goading Sommerfeld into stuff, and he recalled the two of them talking intensely at the Political Science Department party where he had been chastised for being a "swisher.".

Sabina had pressed him about this guy. All Simon could come up with was that he, too, had something to do with computer science at Penn or at least was known to the other grads there. He couldn't recall a specific name, though he thought it was something like "Barnstone."

Sabina's first step, even ahead of contacting Russell, was to see if University of Pennsylvania or other Philadelphia sources unearthed anything about any 'Barnstone' sounding name back in the late sixties and early seventies. For that information, someone had to look through hard paper records from back then. She knew just the person.

She played phone tag for a few days with her high school friend Heidi Dietrich, now an Assistant Librarian at Temple University. She finally got through two nights later and arranged the research Heidi would need to do. Heidi was herself into doing a little bit of sleuthing.

Heidi went to the University of Pennsylvania main library and poured through the collections and archives for 1968-1971. Then, she accessed an enrollment list for the same period. While she was at it, she went through the Philadelphia newspapers for the same period. They had just been keyworded for searches.

Heidi had found nothing after a couple of weeks on and off. Then two things caught her attention. An anti-war protest variant combining "Hey, Hey LBJ, How Many Kids Are You Going to Kill Today!" with Ho, Ho Chi Minh, the NLF is Going to Win!" that had attracted opposition to the anti-war protest, including a bunch of John Birchers' and a big young guy carrying a sign that said, "Ho, No (Ala)Mo!" A bravery equal to the Alamo defense was being attributed by many anti-war demonstrators to the North Vietnamese regime. The sign seemed like a Texas angle in the anti-protest. In the text of the article, the same big guy was asked what his sign meant. He had said, "The Alamo's victims were heroic. Those Commies in Viet Nam aren't like that. They murder everyone, including their own. They crush any individualism. I'm angry that so many Americans can't see that."

The guy refused to identify himself, but the article named him with some of the other Birchers. The name stood out to Heidi. The guy's name was Carter Bairstow.

Maybe close enough to "Barnstorm." Bairstow had received an undergraduate degree at Penn in 1968, but she could only find one more item for that name in Philadelphia over that period. Lo and behold, he showed up in a more famous photo in 1970. Apparently, he had turned his attention away from the Birchers' concerns to police anti-protest activities. He had been photographed holding a sign "Pigs Can Fry!"

Heidi phoned Sabina and gave her the name and the background she had dug up on Bairstow from the late 60s in Philadelphia.

"That's great, Heidi. Sounds like even then, he was a wild and crazy guy. If you get a chance, you might check out Drexel or Temple – he may have still been on the university scene in Philadelphia, even if not at Penn itself."

Sabina asked Russell to check out the name Carter Bairstow. He found only one item, but it did the trick. It seems one Carter Bairstow had indeed been once a John Bircher. Its activities then included the distribution of literature critical of civil rights legislation, warnings over the influence of the United Nations, and the release of petitions to impeach United States Supreme Court Justice Earl Warren. The John Birchers, at that point, also bragged that it was impossible for opponents of the society to infiltrate it, thereby protecting it from "anti-American" infiltrators.

Bairstow re-entered the Bircher picture as part of a small group of break-away Birchers in Austen, Texas, in 1975 who had then actually claimed the main society had indeed been infiltrated by left-wing agent provocateurs, causing America in reaction to become more extreme than necessary. Bairstow and his few dissenting Bircher colleagues called for a more measured extremism – kind of an oxymoron, mindful of Goldwater, she thought. But then, probably many Birchers were morons. The difference was on the race issues related to civil rights. Bairstow was among very few Society members at the time who apparently thought Afro-Americans could be both good Americans and good John Birchers.

Nothing else about Bairstow. Russell was surprised - why would someone that bold and with that profile already simply disappear from history?

Sabina thought, maybe a name change. It would take some sleuthing in Houston.

She had an opportunity. In the past summer, she had spent a three-month period between May and August as an articling junior assistant at the International Court of Justice in The Hague. Among the interesting persons she had met, she had along well with an American ad hoc appointee from Texas just completing his term there. He had just left the ICJ, and she found out he was back in Austin. On a hunch. she picked up the phone and contacted the guy. He was there and would love to meet Sabina for lunch.

She flew down that night, and they were at lunch the next day.

The man she looked at, Brandon Thomas, was middle age. It was very hot, and he was sweating a bit. So was she.

"It's been in the high 90's and 100's here for three weeks. We sometimes get a break in Austen. Not this fall. Anyway, Sabina, what brings you here?"

"Well, I first have a few questions about my nomination for a permanent position with the ICJ."

"I'd be delighted to try and answer them for you." He was very good at providing some key background details. He threw in a few of the best places to live in The Hague if she should return there.

"I am grateful for all that. Thanks so much."

"Not at all."

"I must confess there was one other matter that brought me to you."

"Oh, what's that?"

"I think something that can only be followed up here. There's a guy – someone who was a Bircher back in the 70s who was one of those claiming Society had been penetrated by Communist provocateurs that had made it more extreme than necessary. His name then was Carter Bairstow. I can't find anything on him since. I think he may have since changed his name."

"What's your interest, if I may ask?"

"He was at university with Simon Kiss, a close friend in Toronto who has developed some amazing computer-assisted strategy gaming innovations. We are looking for him to see where he's at now," Sabina said.

"Well, as an African American, I was quite aware of that guy back in the seventies. He was one of the few Birchers who seemed to separate right-wing stuff from race stuff. He was even saying that Blacks could be good Birchers. I mean, that was sure a new line. Anyway, he led a few break-away Birchers for a while. And then, as you say, he seemed to disappear. A year later, I was an assistant in the State Attorney's office, and a person of interest came up in a case. There was a photo. It was Bairstow. But a different name."

"What was the new name?"

"Karl Maddow. He had become an oil industry consultant, and he was a friend of a still active murder case victim. The police cleared him of any connection to the murder, which was never solved. I was initially suspicious of the guy and wondered a bit about him. He had seemed to make such an abrupt change in his life. He told us that he had too negative a profile as a Bircher, even among most Birchers, so he had to make a clear break, even changing his name. I still think there was something not quite right about him. I wanted the police to ask him more questions, but they didn't press anything. I can't give you anything after that. I've never heard of Maddow again. Does that name help?"

"Well, not yet, but that's been most helpful. I can see if there are later references. For starters, where's Austin's main library?"

"I've got some time. I'll take you there. We can use their new fully automated microfiche. I can also see if there are any subsequent official records."

Sabina had found a fellow sleuth.

They parked at (Library), and we're soon searching for anything on Karl Maddow. Thomas called two contacts on his cell phone. Drivers' License had no record of a license issued to that name in the Austin area or State files after 1977. A run on the social security number and crime database would later provide no record on Carter Bairstow after 1974 and nothing on a Karl Maddow."

"That's nine years incognito," marveled Thomas.

"We think he is still a guy somehow in the Houston oil industry community."

Thomas said, "Maybe he changed his name again. It's still been years since we have a record. He could be anywhere now, under yet another new name."

"Okay. The only thing we can do now is start a profile on him. I'll get that done by a good private investigator, I know. You've been a terrific help, Brandon. I'll keep you posted. If you think of anything, please contact me."

"Will do," he said as he deposited her at the Austin airport.

Chapter 36

Sabina thought little of return air flights on the same day, but she was tired when she finally entered the front door of her apartment in Toronto and went to bed.

The next morning, she contacted Russell to meet her for lunch in the bar at the King Edward, down the street from her condo.

Russell slipped into her booth at 12:30, and they both ordered appletinis and a burger.

They clinked glasses, and Russell asked, "What's up?"

Sabina filled him in on her sleuthing in Texas.

"A cold trail," he concluded for her. "The name we got for him didn't last long."

"Right. So, I think we won't have a newer or current name for quite a while. What I'd like is for you to use your profiling contact to work up a profile on this guy. Maybe more than one. It might really help to finally solve the Keefe and Davies murders and in case the guy ever shows up again to haunt Simon."

"Could do that. But that'll cost you – not for me but for the profiler. Probably at least $10,000."

"Money well spent. Go ahead with it, please, Russ."

"Will do."

Two nights later, Sabina was looking at the profiler's initial report. She thought Simon would be interested when he got back.

She especially liked the summary.

"Big guys are noticeable from childhood, whether they like it or not. They usually try to develop ways of being less noticeable. But, if they start doing big things, they stick out more than ever. Apparently, this guy wants to do big things, big time, and not be noticed, at least not later. Hence, change of name, but that's drastic. So, the big things could be very big. Attached is a worked-up picture of what he might look like now from the last photos we have."

Sabina looked at the likeness and didn't see anyone like that she could remember seeing in recent years. Maybe Simon would.

Maybe though, if the last name change had been recent, they might recognize the guy in Texas, in the office where people could process a change in their name.

Karl Maddow looked down at his new name on the real estate documents on his desk in the library of his new home: William Barry Jones. It didn't have a ring to it. It was a common name but not too obviously common, like John Smith. It had an impenetrable documentary background, not anything remotely Texan. Among his many talents, he was as pleased with his ability to assume and thoroughly document a new name as he was with his ability to extinguish an old one. By now, he was very good at it. After all, it was his third assumed name.

He looked out the window wall at the Pacific Ocean, that portion of it lying off Vancouver over Burrard Inlet from the Strait of Georgia. The sun was setting in the west. Its long shadows helped him pick out several waiting ships in those outer reaches of Vancouver harbor.

They would never find him here. And they would never know when his younger self had finally forged into steel his singular purpose in life to seek and destroy socialism.

He had once flirted with socialism when he was infatuated by Donna Mayer. It wasn't enough to be working with some super-rich oil czars on a strategic plan for a new world capitalism, one that would be run by a permanent Republican majority in America. What he seriously disliked in Simon Kiss became the hate that he had developed for Donna, Simon's wealthy and carelessly leftist girlfriend at Penn.

His mind went back to July 1970.

He was on the 1-95, driving his brand new Suburban south of Rocky Mount, North Carolina. He was following an old Dodge Dart beater that was carrying Donna and some Yippie friends to meet their Weathermen contacts for a bit of anti-war violence at Duke.

More precisely, he was following Simon Kiss in his late model Riviera, who was following Donna.

He let Simon's car pass the Dart and saw no other vehicles close behind him. He quickly moved out into the passing lane. He could see Donna in the front seat. She was turned toward the others in the rear seats. She had an arm spread out, no doubt emphasizing to her fellow travelers the strategic brilliance of their mission. She had a whiskey bottle in her hand. Then, she saw him passing, and her jaws dropped. He knew she knew. He sideswiped them with cool efficiency. Idiots, he thought.

It had taken him only a few days after that to accept he had killed some people. He was likely going to have to kill some more people. The only way to deal with a stupid world, he had thought at the time and since.

His telephone buzzed.

"Yes." he said.

"Good evening, Mr. Jones. Somebody suggested I contact you. I may have something you'd be interested in.

Name?

"Bill Stephens. People call me Red."

"Never heard of you, sorry."

"Okay. Understood. Let me hang up, and I'll ring again and put something on your voicemail. You may wish to contact me after you have listened to what I say."

"Doubtful, but what's this about?"

"There is someone in Houston who thinks you should talk to me."

"Would that be Houston, in Texas? I don't know anyone in Houston. Who could that be?"

"Barnet Williams."

Williams was his billionaire buddy, helping fund the big stuff.

"I don't have time for prank calls." Maddow rang off.'

When the call came in, though, he thought he better find out more. He let it go to voice mail and listened.

"So, here's the thing: Mr. Williams knows where you are and doesn't want to let you go so easily. He wanted more from you to keep working out the future of the elephant. Anyway, he wants you for at least another year, as you proposed. Do not let him down. I can meet you on the observation deck of the Harbor Centre Tower tomorrow morning at 11:00 a.m. I have red hair. I will recognize you. Don't be late, please."

Okay, I thought Williams might not let me go so easily, thought Maddow. The only guy who has the resources, smarts, and reason to chase me this far. Maddow knew he should have cut that tie better. It had been too hot in Toronto and too urgent; he just didn't have the time.

At precisely 11:00 the next morning, Maddow walked out onto the observation deck of the Vancouver Harbor Centre Tower. He headed to a red-haired man looking through the binoculars. They then looked at his watch and said, "Right on time, Karl."

"Well, I never meant to abandon Barnett. I am pleased to make good to him. What more does he want?"

"As it happens, nothing."

"What do you mean?"

"I'm not going to do the explaining. The lady approaching us will."

Both men watched as Sabina Hurst joined them.

She smiled but declined Maddow's proffered handshake.

"I am afraid I am not at all pleased to meet you Maddow. You see, Simon Kiss is my very good friend. As it happens, I have developed my talent for sleuthing in my law training and assisted my Hurst family's PI here, Red Stephens, who is, in fact, Rusty Russell, Toronto PI extraordinaire. Together, we got to your influencer, and after some tussling back and forth, he reluctantly shared with us the information only his own operatives could gather about your latest move, Maddow. Power on Power. Money on Money, as it were. A Queen was left on the Board, with a King in an exposed position. Anyway, the jig's up for you, Maddow,

"Spoken like a gumshoe in a 40s movie," said Maddow. "But, you see, you are confused. I am not who you say. I have just moved down here from Prince George, where I was last. I'm a mining engineer. Folks, remember me up there. It will be apparent in the records."

"Well, we already knew you were very good at cut-outs. I must admit that was masterful in Prince George. A guy who looked like you had gone missing in the mountains. A daring if brief reappearance, and a total confiscation of his identity, with a few bribes here and there. All done in one month. Brilliant, if no one else figured out what you were doing. But we did. So now, it's all going to collapse on you."

"Again, I don't know what you're talking about. Either of you. Go tell it to the police or whomever. In the meantime, good morning to you both."

Maddow strode angrily off the observation deck to the elevators.

Where he was met by three waiting Mounties, putting him under arrest for suspicion of murder and espionage.

A week later, on a rainy December Friday, a still bandaged Simon was visited at Lesliehurst by Chief Inspector Miservy.

Shown into the conservatory, Simon waved Miservy to sit down. They looked at each other for a few moments, neither quite sure how to start the conversation.

Simon finally said, "Basically, it turned out I blamed myself for something Maddow did, and then Sommerfeld allowed himself to exploit the resulting split of my personality since 1971. I never realized I was so mentally vulnerable until the obstacle course at Worlds."

"Okay, you can continue to relax a recover here," said Miservy. "We interviewed Sommerfeld at length the day before he took his own life. He explained that he had been given a very powerful tool last university year by a professor of Psychiatry at Penn with whom he shared leftist views. He confessed, Simon, that you were a perfect subject after Donna's death and thought he had good reason to use it on you ever since. "

"I wonder if he realized the harm he was doing to me? And three persons - no, six persons - are dead because of his influence on events."

"Well, Simon, he committed suicide, so I would answer on his behalf – yes. Sommerfeld said he was ashamed and stricken with guilt, even though he stressed to me he had no advance knowledge of any of those deaths, though he was sure by then the Toronto deaths were caused by the unknown people he reported to."

Miservy glanced at his notes. He said, *"All I ever said to Davies was an obvious caution – make sure no one saw him pilfer the tape. When Davies sent it back to you, I thought I had to report to the group. I got a message back indirectly that the group might have to withdraw from Toronto; everyone had to evaluate how hot the fact of the stolen tape was. Sommerfeld admitted to arranging the mortar shelling on Halloween at your farm and his own attempt to find out what he could about the latest back game with the Soviet military and maybe get more access to or information about your computer core tape."*

Simon was still not convinced.

"Well, here's a short note he wrote to you." Miservy handed the note to Simon.

"Simon, I am very sorry - I have long since lost my juvenile envy of you, and I certainly no longer trust the network I have been foolishly a part of and that you yourself unwittingly sent information to at some points. I can only say I have cut ties with them. But I warn you, they may still be around. Take care. My long-term hope for wonderful non-military uses of Rondo is the same as yours."

Simon shook his head slowly.

"You make me want to feel sorry for Sommerfeld- after all the shit he did, however indirectly."

"Well, he took his own life because of that, Simon. And you are now released from that by your own brave actions. "

"And," said Simon, "Sabina and Russell finally traced everything to King Maddow, that son of a bitch who got Sommerfeld to do his bid as early as that long-ago grad party at Penn.

"Yes. I guess. Thanks for sharing this, Inspector."

The new houseman entered, saying, "Telephone call for you, Inspector."

Miservy took the call, beginning to smile. He ended the call.

"Maddow was too smart by half, heading to Vancouver - no need for extradition from the States, though he claims his true identity is an American citizen. He's managed to retain one of our top criminal lawyers for his defense, but the court just refused bail," he said to Simon.

The two men happily bid good afternoon.

Chapter 37

The logs were burning brightly in the huge library fireplace at Lesliehurst. The Hurst family was gathered at Christmas 1983 and enjoying the first moments of peace in a long time.

Simon could finally begin to relax after ending two back channels – the one with the Pentagon and his personal one.

Earl and Amy were fussing about after bringing in the wines and traditional roasted chestnuts, asparagus rolls, cheeses, and *foie gras* that the Hursts had long enjoyed in the appetizer platters on Christmas Eve. Later a dinner buffet featuring roast goose would be served on a special refectory table brought up from the cellars expressly for Christmas Eve.

Roy and Leandra Hurst, as usual, presided. Their son, Phillip, had flown in from Vancouver. Sabina and Simon sat together on one of the sofas. Ivan Tarasov was smiling at everyone, regaling them with Russian Christmas tales and telling them delightedly that this moment for him at Lesliehurst was superb. A few close neighbors had joined them, along with several of those who provided various services to the Hurst family and tended the estate. It was, as always, a fulsomely attended and most merry evening. It became merrier.

At one moment, there was a knock at the door. There stood The Ontario Premier's executive assistant, Les Lovett, followed by two uniformed gentlemen carrying a large gift-wrapped square box. It was addressed to Simon.

As they joined the group in a Christmas toast, the present was set down, and Simon tore away at the wrapping and opened the box. The protective cardboard fell away and revealed a large music box with several dancers, who, when Lovett pressed a button for the toy performance to begin, began a dance that Simon immediately identified as a Rondo.

"Lovett said, "Here is the Premier's card to you.

"*To Simon Kiss: Best of the season to you and all yours. I hope someday you may receive an Order of Ontario, but I think this is a more meaningful gift on behalf of an appreciative Province! Our new Deputy Minister of Development sourced it from a friend in Germany. Paid for by staff voluntary donations, I might add – no exchange gift must ever be sent, or we'll all be in trouble!*"

"Oh, please thank the Premier, and the others who did this, Les." said Simon. "This is a most meaningful and exquisite gift. I will place it beside my desk and play it often."

Long after the dinner and when good nights and Merry Christmas had been said and said again, the immediate Hurst family was left to enjoy alone together for their final waking hour after midnight.

Port was poured, and heads turned to Sabina and Simon.

Sabina looked as every head turned to her and said, "We shall be married in June. Here."

This brought a noisy éclat from the rest of the family and its long-serving staff.

"Oh, get the best champagne – but wait, is any chilled," said Roy Hurst.

Earl said, "I have a secret. Amy and I already knew why the best had to be chilled and waiting!"

Everyone milled about kissing and hugging until the champagne was brought in and poured.

Roy Hurst offered the toast.

"I cannot tell you, Sabina and Simon, how thrilled Leandra and I are at this news. You are a match, a wondrous match. Let us drink to Simon and Sabina and then hugs all round for all present and future Kisses!"

They all clinked glasses.

Tarasov, treated now as one of the family, added, "To life!"

They all clinked glasses again.

Phillip said, "Please fill me in on the latest. The last I heard, even Dad might be headed for jail."

Simon said, "Well, yes, this is the first time we can fill all of you in on all that has happened in the last few weeks."

The family gathered around.

"When I recovered my memory of the contacts I had made over the years in a dissociative state with David Sommerfeld, I was in shock for a few days - imagine almost completely losing a side of yourself for over a decade."

There were murmurs of sympathy.

"When all that had sunk in and I was steady enough - I cannot emphasize enough how helpful Dr. Ansfer was at Worlds, and Sabina most of all at that point. At the Don Jail, before he took his own life, Sommerfeld verified my recent recall of all the contacts with him and how he had put them into action in ways I did not know with people who, for the most part, even he did not know, based on a cryptic advertisement in Decision and Theory back in 1974 seeking new tools for global social change and policy making. As it turned out, I have been feeding that network, via Sommerfeld, too many details about Rondo ever since. And they took grievous advantage of that trying to get to my Rondo gaming core here in Toronto."

The family collectively nodded their understanding.

"Now, with Dr. Ansfer's counsel, I have recovered that lost memory, and more to the point, I am now equipped with methods to avoid any further mental separation of different sides of my psyche. I am finally free in every sense to pursue a full range of non-military global strategy applications and development of the Rondo software."

He looked around at everyone, still not quite finished.

"Indeed, I am rid of two risky back channels, the military one and, even more essential, my own personal one that long split me."

The family applauded.

Sabina said, "Simon would never have permitted Russ and me to take down the big guy. But hey, we did! And I am even happier to declare that all sides of the two of us welcome our upcoming marriage!"

Even greater applause.

Simon lifted his glass and said, "To my precious Sabina. Sleuth of this or any other year!"

They all raised their glasses and lustily cheered again.

Roy Hurst made the final toast.

"Let me offer a toast to advancing sound and humane global policy – and to this wonderful coming marriage of Sabina and Simon and much else good in the world!"

Simon and Sabina embraced as Simon flipped the switch on the music box. The dancers again danced the refraining rondo music to the spheres of human strategy.

www.ingramcontent.com/pod-product-compliance
Lightning Source LLC
Chambersburg PA
CBHW041315110526
44591CB00021B/2797